Priceless Success Principles

Proven Principles To Take Control Of Your Life

By Craig Price

ISBN: 146795294X
ISBN 13: 9781467952941

Table Of Contents

Preface

This book is for people who have always wanted more out of life but never thought it was possible for them. The principles I share in this book will give you the blueprint to success and happiness and will save you years of struggling and hard work and you'll achieve all your dreams and desires by applying my tried and tested principles

I have helped thousands of people to live their life of their dreams and live free from the barriers or boundaries that once held them back. Your life and your time on this planet is precious we all know how quickly time flies by. The biggest waste of your life and the biggest waste of your own individual time is spending years on trying to attain something you could have achieved in only a matter of weeks or months.

By following the proven strategies and methodologies in Priceless Success Principles in this book for setting your Priceless Life and living your dream you will achieve your dreams in a much faster and productive manner than you could ever have imagined before and people and family and friends will be amazed by the transformations in you.

In my one to one therapy and life coaching and seminars and I have worked with thousands of people who have found consistently that it doesn't matter what your upbringing, your education or your own individual talents if these principle are followed then success will also follow

This book contains my secrets that I have learned over the last 15 years on success, achievement and controlling that little voice inside your head or what I like to call the Dominating, Delusional Destructive Dragon.

By following the steps and principles in this book and the pages that I'm excited for you to read, you will not only get on the road or the pathway to greatness but you'll also have the key to open the door to your own individual greatness.

If I can do it anyone can

About 15 years ago, I started to get really serious and focused about all the things I'd always wanted in life. I soon realised that what I had been doing for all these years hadn't been working and if my life was to change I had to change dramatically.

I started to invest in myself and in my future by learning everything I could of how the subconscious mind works. I spent hours and hours researching why I had done what I had done for all these years and why I continued to do it even when it wasn't working for me.

I put together a plan a road map to success that just worked, all the best and easiest to apply ideas that did change my life with huge results and easy to apply principles. I began by applying it into my life and really quickly I went from arguing for my limitations and making up 101 excuses of why I couldn't do it, to finding new and exciting ways of performing much more effectively and productively in every area of my life.

What I soon found was these principles work all the time for everyone regardless of your education, abilities or even upbringing. I learned that my principles I had set in place had taken me from a life of fear, procrastination, frustration, underachievement blaming my situation on everyone and everything else to a place of success and feeling great about and proud of myself.

I soon learned that the limitations I had were self imposed on my own abilities I thought I had at that time. I knew that millions of people had started with absolutely nothing and attained awesome success in their lives and I knew if they could do it then so could I.

About Craig Price

Craig Price is an Advanced Psychotherapist, Celebrity Life Coach, Motivational Speaker, Personal Development Expert and Author, creator of The Priceless Success Principles Program and Mental Health Mechanics Program and the Elite Psychotherapist for Visual Coding Displacement Therapy and Schema Conditioning Psychotherapy for the U.K. and has helped thousands of clients live free from their challenges or mental health issues that once held them back, clients who hire Craig say he's a dream giver and could never of thought it was possible to achieve their dreams without Craig's help.

Craig believes that it's our own individual programming that changes our lives for the better or for the worse, which Craig calls the viruses that have been installed into our subconscious minds or the Dominating Delusional Destructive Dragon (which is his pet name for it) at an early age which must be addressed to change your life for the better.

You can find out more about Craig and his Psychotherapy & Coaching Sessions & products at:

www.pricelesssuccess.com
www.pricelesstherapy.com
www.pricelessweightloss.com
www.billionairebeliever.com

Foreword

We first met Craig many years ago when he came to see us in our private practice, Craig had a fantastic life, but he wanted more. He had achieved great things, he was happy, healthy, had a beautiful family and he ran a very successful business but he knew that he could have more and he could offer others far more than he could in his current career.

It is a very rare occurrence when you meet someone and immediately know what they were destined to do in life, we had that moment with Craig. Craig is a born motivator, he not only motivates he also walks the walk as well. There are so many coaches and motivators in the world today who hypocritically offer you a promise of a magic ticket to greatness when their own lives are a complete mess. Craig didn't just wake up one day and think that would be a good career choice for him, it was what he was always meant to do and he is testimony to everything he professes and he is quite literally living his own personal dreams.

Craig has utilised techniques that we taught him so many years ago, used them to enhance his own life and with the benefit of his further experience he now has an array of amazing tools available to him that will very quickly enhance anybody's life. Craig, like ourselves, has an uncontrollable passion for wanting to make a change and he knows that the only thing stopping anyone from achieving greatness is the story they have made up as to why they cannot or why they are not worthy to do so.

In this book he will share with you some of the most fabulous techniques in the world of personal change available today, techniques that will quite literally transform your world, open doors and offer you a life with opportunities you previously could only ever imagine. Which all leads you to the start of your journey and the most important question of all, a question which if answered correctly, will literally change your life forever!

Do you really want it?

Nik & Eva Speakman
Celebrity Life Coaches & Psychotherapists, Creators of Visual Coding Displacement Therapy & Schema Conditioning Psychotherapy.

Introduction

We are living in the most awesome time of our lives, our worries or issues aren't what they used to be back hundreds of years ago, our issues we deal with aren't avoiding getting shot or avoiding being bitten by a bug that can kill you or avoiding saying something so the government will behead you.

We don't deal with those issues anymore; we are dealing with our own individual issues of self realisation. That is the game we play with ourselves that is our issue. Our biggest bugbear in life is our mind, which I like to call The Dominating Delusional Destructive Dragon which is the start of all our suffering, our very own perspective on the world, we don't deal with the problems of having to protect ourselves from the world or challenges that once were an issue to people hundreds of years ago thanks to the advancements in medical science and education.

Everyone is trying to protect themselves from "_what if_" and "_if only_", the two words _what_ and the word _if_ mean nothing on their own, but place them together and they can open up a whole world of opportunities for you, or close a million doorways it's just a case of how you perceive it in your own individual mind.

This book will show you how to stop protecting yourself so you can live free from those shackles that once held you back and _what if,_ will mean endless opportunities and possibilities for you.

Before we begin on your life transformation, I want to congratulate you on taking that first step that will lead you towards breaking new boundaries in your life.

I'm sure you'll agree as humans there's areas in our lives where we want and deserve more out of life, and there are also areas of our lives that you would wish to improve for the better. It could even be a habit or a behavioural pattern that you would simply love to change but somehow all your attempts and actions in the past to change just don't seem to work.

Why is it that some people enjoy better health, happier relationships, greater success in their careers, and achieve financial independence and great wealth while others don't.

What is it that enables some people to accomplish remarkable things and enjoy wonderful lives while so many others feel frustrated and disappointed?

Think back over the past couple of months or years. How many times have your fear or procrastination or self doubt or your excuses you use, stopped you from succeeding?
I'm here to tell you. It doesn't have to be this way for you anymore.

There is a formula to overcoming this fear, procrastination and self doubt and you can learn precisely how to develop your own Priceless Success Principles that will lead you straight to the life you've always desired and deserved.

If fear has ever stopped you from asking for a raise, starting a business, asking for a date or simply interacting with people during daily activities, you're not alone. It happens to all of us all of the time, however a great saying to remember is if you do what you've always done you will always get the same old results.

No one starts off poised and confident in every situation. Fortunately, self confidence and self esteem is a learned behaviour. And I can teach you in this working life program, Priceless Success principles which are proven principles that just work if you follow the formula.

People just like you are now living the lives they've always dreamed of because they have mastered the Priceless Success Principles. When you develop your Priceless Success Principles, everything else just falls into place. So if you're serious about success, THIS is the place to start. Begin your new life and let the transformations begin.

When I was a teenager I started to wonder, what was the difference between those who seemed to succeed in every aspect of their lives? People who are great spouses, great business people, good with money, great parents, great communicators, great talkers, great listeners and so on?

I would often think, "What's the difference between them and me? What decisions or choices have they made or what lucky breaks have they had that allows them to live in big posh houses and drive nice cars? Can I have these things one day or am I doomed to just struggle through all of my life?" I made a choice one day as a teenager that I was going to one day live the good life. I wasn't going to live in poverty. My family would be able to have whatever they wanted. I was never going to tell my children that we could not afford something.

The only problem was that I didn't know how to attain these things. The only person that I knew was a friend of mine who I worked for, who had all the things I had always wanted. He became the image of what I wanted to be. I wanted to drive nice cars, wear nice clothes and live in a big posh house in the countryside.

That's when I knew what I really wanted; the only challenge was I had to figure out how to get it. I had always dreamed of being my own boss and running my own business. So I began watching and looking into and up to successful people and I began to research and read everything I could about them and how they did it.

I attended loads of seminars and read books and listened to audio programmes. At every opportunity I could I made sure every day was a school day so I could learn something new to continuously move me forward to my dream life.

This process was obviously overwhelming at times, but I found common traits, principles and patterns that all these successful people had in common. So I started to implement these principles and traits into my life over 14years ago. These principles helped me to start multiple businesses, gain balance in my life, maintain motivation and focus and reach massive goals that I set for myself that I thought I could never have achieved before.

I have now had the pleasure to teach and coach thousands of clients to experience the same results in their own lives. Now let me first start by saying, this isn't easy if it was then everyone in the world would be successful, however if you follow the principles in this book they will provide you with the fundamentals, methodologies and the secret ingredients that will inspire and motivate you towards your very own Priceless Life. A bit like a life success manual that you incorporate into your life each and everyday and make each and every change that's necessary, then you will be on your very own journey to the new you.

If you are ready to start living that life you've always wanted, dreamed of and always desired, keep reading and join the thousands of others who are doing the same.

So what is this book is all about, it's all about how to control that subconscious mind of ours, so it will work for us in a more productive manner, so we can get things done and no longer be imprisoned by our negative thoughts that we hold onto that we've allowed to control our lives.

Now don't get me wrong, I know this feels like a weird concept or a lot of hard work, but I promise you, if you follow the formula and work consistently on your goal to improve yourself and your circumstances, then everything that you've always wanted will be yours. I know how I felt when I first tried it, it seems strange, and that's just natural because everything new seems strange for the first few times. But I'm sure you've had tons of experiences in the past when you tried something new that felt weird and after a few days or weeks just became the normal way of doing things.

What I had discovered has amazed me and I realised that I wanted to share this new knowledge with everyone, everyday I see people who can benefit from this. My life changed dramatically when I discovered the secrets I'm going to share with you in this book, I have enjoyed experiences and opportunities that most people can only dream about. I am blessed with a wonderful family life, we live in the beautiful Shropshire countryside in England and I have a lifestyle that I previously have thought could never be mine, I help people to live life to the full with my Psychotherapy and Life Coaching Practise and watching clients change their own lives and live free from depression, panic/anxiety attacks, fears and phobias truly is an awesome pleasure.

What I will share with you in this book is my proven techniques, principles and strategies to improve your life, to help you make positive changes and results in all areas from your career and business to your health and fitness and your relationships and even boosting your confidence and self esteem.

If you're anything like I was living in a perpetual Monday morning syndrome, with an argument for everything of why you just can't do it. Making up reasons upon reasons of why it's so hard to do and only the educated and select few become successful, then this is for you.

If I can do it anyone can, so are you ready to start being the new you and ready to make the journey to your new life where it can be priceless for you too?

When I started to get really serious and focused about all the things I'd always wanted in life. I soon realised that what I had been doing for all these years hadn't been working and if my life was to change I had to change dramatically.

We're on this together I'll coach and guide you through the whole process of this rollercoaster ride called life so hang on and lets get started.

It's never too late to be who you might be. Make that decision today to be all you can be.

Craig Price

The Day My Life Changed

For most people to change something drastic has to happen to them such as an overweight person is told by the doctor if he doesn't change his eating and exercising habits then he'll become diabetic and wont see his daughter get married because he simply wont be around long enough for it to happen.

For me it was about fifteen years ago I was running my own small business just plodding along, just about paying the bills when suddenly a company I'd done business with for a long time went into receivership owing me lots of money. Money which I was counting on to pay my bills and my suppliers and my mortgage, this consequently took me into my overdraft with very little money left in fact there was only £300 left in my overdraft.

So if you're reading this book and you have more than £5 in your purse or wallet, that's more money than I had when I first started my journey.

I did what most young men would do, I went to my parents to see if they could lend me some money to help me overcome this sticky patch I'd entered into (one which I kept telling myself wasn't my fault) my parents said if I needed it they could lend me £1,000 but that's it.

I vowed to myself that I would get myself out of this sticky situation on my own, and would do whatever it took to make it happen. And I would do it all on my own without any monetary help from my parents, so I got to work and started working on myself. I soon realised that we all live our lives stuck in habits, routines, and belief systems that have brought us to where we are in life today. Our thoughts, behaviours and habits and routines are to blame for where we are right now....

The things that we believe to be true determine are Thoughts, Feelings, Actions and Behaviours, or what I now call our T.F.A.B...

I started to knock on more and more doors and each time I had a no, I moved on to the next until I found enough people that could buy my products and services. Every no from a potential client I thought to myself was getting me closer to a yes from another client (see how my thought process had changed in a very short time)

My Mum bought me a personal development cd that I listened to for about 15 minutes in my car. I thought it was a load of garbage all about how this guy had transformed his life and stopped listening to other people and how he'd become successful. After 15 minutes I turned it off and basically said to myself huh, as if I want to listen to this rubbish and I didn't listen to it for at least another week or so.

But something this guy had said made me curious, what he had done to turn his life around. So I listened to it again and most importantly I took action (which is the most powerful 6 letter word in the dictionary) on what he said and things, situations and my circumstances in my life started to change

I remember the day my life changed, I'd been working on myself and my business for a while and I was making consistent and persistent changes in my life and business. I was starting to turn things around and I could see light at the end of the tunnel. I was becoming successful.

I started to become really interested in the subconscious mind and how it works and why we do what we do or even, why we don't do what we must do. I took my exams in Psychotherapy and Nero Linguistic Programming and as I'm writing this book in 2011 at the age of 41 I'm now an advanced Psychotherapist and The Elite Psychotherapist and Life Coach for Visual Coding Displacement Therapy and Schema Conditioning Psychotherapy for the creators Nik and Eva Speakman, who since meeting them 10 years ago have taken me under their wing and introduced me to a whole new world of how the subconscious mind works, who I'm both eternally grateful for.

I learnt whatever I could and listened to any self development program I could get my hands on and learnt as much new stuff as often as I could. The day it all changed for me, how I turned everything around was when one day with everything that I'd learnt about how the subconscious minds works. I was in an industrial estate, sat in a car park looking at all the different businesses and deciding which businesses I could sell my products and services to.

Each and every business could have bought my products and services and I actually caught myself doing something that I had done for numerous years before and had never known I was doing. (and I'll explain later on in the book how and why this works), As I'm sure you all know we talk to ourselves everyday in fact experts say we talk to ourselves every 11 seconds. Anyway I was deciding which companies I would endeavour to sell my products and services to, and I caught myself saying. I'll knock on that company door and that one and that one but I won't knock on that one.

I stopped myself and asked myself the question "why is it ok to knock on those company doors and sell my products and services but not that door." Now when you ask yourself a good question you come up with a great answer, and the little voice inside my head said "because I'm not confident to knock on that door" now with all my new found knowledge of how the subconscious mind worked, I asked myself another question so I could get to the root cause of why.

"Why am I not confident to knock on that particular door" and remember when you ask yourself a great question you come up with a great answer and my little voice said "because that's a big business and I'm confident to knock on small companies doors, but not on big companies doors."

I continued to ask myself questions, so I thought to myself there must be a reason why my confidence levels are high when it comes to small companies and very low or non existent when it comes to big businesses.

Quick as a flash my mind said "big businesses don't do business with small companies." Again I asked myself another question "is that really true." I thought of the biggest company I could think of at the time and it was Virgin, which was owned by Richard Branson, and I asked myself another great question "does Virgin deal with small companies" yes they do, in fact one of Virgins and Richard Branson's core values is to help out budding entrepreneurs who are just starting out in business.

After having the realisation that for all these years I believed in something that just simply wasn't true, but it had made me think, feel, act and behave in a certain way, which had cost me financially.

I realised that everyone believes in certain things or aspects of their lives that aren't true, because it's all locked up inside our subconscious minds. Until we question our beliefs and see them for what they really are, just stupidity that we let control our habits, routines and actions, and we'll always stay in the same place and never move forward in life.

That realisation I had that day with all the new learning's I had started to apply into my life, changed my life forever.

What Are The Priceless Success Principles?

It's all about how to control that subconscious mind of ours, (or our dominating, delusional, destructive dragon which is what I like to call it, and we'll cover this later on in the book) so it will work for us in a more productive manner, so we can get things done and no longer be imprisoned by our negative thoughts that we hold onto that we've allowed to control our lives.

Now in many ways we want to change, but our mind doesn't want to get out of its comfort zone. It will tell you things like: "there's no need to do that. You know all of this stuff. I'll start it tomorrow. I'm just far too busy now, etc." The mind will come up with all kinds of excuses to convince you not to change or improve your life. If you argue enough for all of your limitations you and your mind will come up with enough excuses or reasons of why you want to keep them. It's a bit like your subconscious mind is the devil or the *"triple d dragon"* which we'll talk more about later on in this book and it's on self destruct to self sabotage you at every opportunity it gets.

I actually have clients that come to see me to help them remove their panic or anxiety attacks, fears or phobias and ask me what type of person they'll be when it's removed and gone. I always say the same thing to clients that ask me this, "isn't the whole idea of making this investment in your life by seeing me today, is to remove these challenges for you, so when they are gone you'll be a much happier and healthier person won't you" and they always say "yes of course it is", I then add "as an intelligent person you couldn't use that as an excuse then could you".

Why does the subconscious mind do this?

Your mind is simply used to things the way they are. It doesn't want to change because it's comfortable where it is and in many ways your mind is happy in its misery. But you're not and the only way things are going to get better is for you to start taking control of your mind and directing your subconscious to create the situations you want in life. This will only happen when you train your mind.

Your Mind Is Similar To An Iceberg

The subconscious is the largest part of our mind. It contains all the messages we've received throughout our lives. It holds millions and millions of thoughts grouped into clusters that form beliefs, mindsets and character traits.

The relationship between the conscious and subconscious minds is like an iceberg. The conscious mind is represented by the visible tip of the portion of the iceberg hidden from view. You can't see the subconscious in action, but it certainly has a major impact on the voyage you take in your life.

The subconscious is the place where all of your learned behaviours reside. Once you learn to walk, you don't need to consider how to lift and place each foot to take the next step, do you? Of course not! Your subconscious mind automatically controls your steps.

When was the last time you thought about breathing? I'm guessing never right, this is because your subconscious mind takes care of this for you on an unconscious level or an automatic pilot basis, just think what life would be like if you had to think about breathing all day, you'd get nothing done would you? You wouldn't even talk, as all you'd be thinking about would be if you've breathed in and out or not.

Your subconscious learns behaviour through repetition and practice. Just as it learned to control your footsteps when you learned to walk, it also controls your footsteps in your life's journey based on what you've reinforced and practised throughout your life.

"The good news is you can reprogram your subconscious mind by inputting and reinforcing new thoughts and actions!"

The greatest discovery of all of human history is the fact that you become what you think about most of the time, the way you think determines the way you react and respond to all sorts of things happening around you, the way you react and respond determines your emotions & your feelings, your emotions determine your actions and your actions determine your behaviours which determine your own results, everything starts with your thinking on the things that you personally believe to be true,

"It's really is as simple as that"

Here's A Quick Exercise You Can Do, To See How Your
Subconscious Mind Plays Tricks On You.

I want to share a simple exercise with you so you can see how your subconscious mind works or how it plays tricks on you, to constantly be that devils voice we all hear. A simple test or exercise is to find a friend or colleague and both get your index finger and touch the tips of your fingers together, right at the fingertips so you've formed a triangle without a base. Just like the image below.

Allow the other person to stroke your finger and their finger from the tips of both of your fingers to the base of the fingers using their thumb and first finger, keep repeating this process, now tell me what are you noticing as you do this?

The really strange thing is you can't tell which one is your finger and which one is the other persons, even when you look at both fingers and you know which one is yours it still feels like one big finger. That's because our subconscious mind plays tricks on us, we don't believe what we see, we see what we believe. The more you keep stroking the fingers it's as if your finger goes numb, our mind is constantly playing tricks with us.

"Your subconscious minds the key to releasing and harnessing your inner greatness"

CHAPTER ONE

Your Priceless Life Destination

Each and every one of us has an endless supply of opportunities and possibilities waiting for us, we just have to stop waiting and start grabbing them.

Craig Price

One of the key principles of success is to have a clear vision of what you want out of life, rather than drifting around aimlessly trying to achieve your dreams. You have to know what you want and desire and focus on it every single day.

The ability to set your goals or your Priceless Life Destination which I like to call it is the Daddy of all skills you can attain, why? Because when you set yourself a destination of where you want to go and what you want to achieve your subconscious mind starts to find new opportunities and different pathways to get there.

It's as if you get drawn to your wants and needs and your subconscious mind is on the lookout trying to find it for you and attract it into your life. Without setting your goals or Priceless Life Destination you will simply just drift through life aimlessly going nowhere. If you don't set a destination for your life you'll quite simply go where the flow and currents of life and other people's experiences and opinions will take you to.

The majority of people in this world believe that they haven't been born into the right family or don't have the right connections and never try. Now the truth is that everyone has so much hidden greatness inside it's scary but we don't apply it to our lives. We are so much better than we think we are its unreal. Whatever you have achieved up to now is a tiny drop in the ocean compared to what is really truly possible for you.

It doesn't matter where you are starting from; the only thing that matters is where you want to go in your life. Your past does not equal your future. Wherever it is you want to go in life is solely determined by your very own individual thoughts of you, your abilities and your own individual barriers that currently stop you and hold you prisoner in your daily life.

When you set yourself a goal not only does it increase your self confidence it also charges up your motivation because when you set a promise to yourself and I mean really set a promise to yourself it's really rare you allow yourself to let yourself down.

When you first start out on your journey the first thing you've got to ask for is what you want, and know where your going and when and how you're going to get there just like when you order a taxi you don't say to the taxi driver just take me anywhere. You have a specific destination to get home or to go to a restaurant the same applies to your life and your dreams you must know your destination and what it will look like when you get there and what getting there will do for you personally.

We've all heard the old saying if you don't ask you don't get. SO LETS START BY ASKING FOR WHAT WE WANT

Create A New Way Of Seeing The World

The number one greatest discovery in the world is that your own mind creates every aspect and every area of your life. Who tells you something is perfect or a load of rubbish? You do, don't you? Only the way you feel about a certain time, place or specific event in your life is determined by your own perception of what it meant to you.

Every invention that we have today that helps us live our lives more effectively was once an idea in someone's head. Every-thing started as a thought or an idea or a dream or a wish. Your life is exactly the same your own thoughts are massively power-ful on your life, they create your own reality and form your own world and every meaning you have or have ever had.

One of the great quotes in philosophy or psychology is you be-come what you think about most of the time. Whatever goes on inside your head is a direct reflection of your own world.

If you think about success and achievement and dreams and goals, it will become your own reality. However if you think about what you don't want and make up enough reasons or excuses of why you can't do it. Or you continuously tell yourself why it's so hard and talk about your problems and your worries. Or con-stantly tell yourself and others why you'll never have what you want because of this and that. It will become your reality.

Living your life without a clear, defined, specific outcome is just like having a blind person help you across the road. No matter how many times he tries he just can't see where he's going and you'll continue to fall into potholes and puddles and oncoming traffic along the road. Having clear goals helps you jump over those potholes and puddles and jump forward massively to your wants and desires.

Remember we all see the world through our own eyes and place a certain amount of significance on certain areas of our lives. Our own perception is our own reality, no ones reality is the same.

Your Built In Satellite Navigation System

Just like a satellite navigation system gets you to your destination every time, you have a built in sat nav with an added bonus that actually attracts your Priceless Life Destination towards you when you have clear defined goals. When you know beyond a shadow of a doubt what you want, you don't have to know how you're going to get it or even where to look for it; you'll just start to move towards your goal and your goal will just start to move towards you, it will feel just like magic.

Let me explain what I mean if your goal is to eat fish and chips and watch television and have a chocolate bar, you will achieve it right? If your goal is to become healthy and exercise regularly so you'll feel better about yourself you'll attain that goal as well. Your goal seeking missile doesn't care what you want, it just gets it on an automatic pilot basis to bring you what you want. It doesn't care if it's good for you or not.

The same thing goes for goal setting; if it's a big goal or a small goal your automatic pilot will help you to achieve big goals or small goals. The decision is up to you, what you want and when you want it.

If Setting Goals is The Answer Why Don't People Do It.?

There are many reasons for this and here's why

People quite simply think it's a load of self help mumbo jumbo and don't take it on board. If you grew up in a household where no one in your family unit set goals or had a clear well drawn out destination for their future. Or your peer group just stroll through life from pay cheque to pay cheque hoping for happiness and success. You'll soon take on their opinions and behavioural patterns. That success trait for setting goals won't even be in your realm of possibilities it just won't even be an option in your head.

Another reason is people just don't know how to do it properly, or they think they know how to do it but really they just have a few "*what if's*" or "*if only's*" in their life, like I want to be rich or I want to be successful, but all they do is just say it and don't take the time in their lives to make it happen. That's more like a wishy washy wish or even a daydream of wanting to make things better for themselves.

A goal is a clear driven destination for what you want and how long it's going to take you, and what you'll have to do and what type of person you'll need to be to accomplish it.

Another reason is people are just scared of failing; they don't set goals because they just don't want that horrible feeling of being a failure. Everyone of has failed at something before in our lives and we don't want anyone to know about it because it will bring disgrace to us. So they go through life never setting goals because they don't want that horrible feeling of being a failure as they feel everyone will be laughing at them. So they continuously go through life living an existence of living at a default setting of mediocrity. Finding evidence and references all day long of why there's no chance it will happen for them.

Setting Goals Gives You a Plan

When you set a goal it gives you something to aim at a bench mark to go for. When you go to work does your boss say to you just do what you want to today? Of course not you have a set plan of what you need to do and by when, setting goals is the same. When you set a goal it gives you a sense of direction in your life and each time you achieve a small step towards your goal it makes you feel happy by having that sense of achievement. Each step towards your goal gives you that certain spring in your step and you start to feel proud of yourself and your accomplishments.

So many people today hate change in their lives, they get so used to doing something in the same way again and again because they become worried about the future and what it will hold for them. When you set a goal it gives you the ability to change and control the direction of your life. The strange thing is with change it happens each and every day but we don't see it. Let me ask you a question are you the same person you were six months ago? If you've said yes I am then you've missed it, everyday we spend on this planet we change physically and mentally as we grow older our own perspective changes.

The Hidden Greatness Within

All of us have so much potential it is scary, everything you've always dreamed of and desired is waiting to jump out of your body and say *"come on give it to me now"* We all have the secret ingredient to attain any goal we desire. You just have to commit to it and set time aside everyday working on it. The more you do this the more that secret ingredient will develop inside of you.

I'm sure you've heard before or even caught yourself saying it to your kids *"if only you just applied yourself that little bit more"* the really sad fact is that we keep it all bottled up waiting and waiting for that one day when we'll need it and then we'll share it with the world. STOP WAITING, unleash your greatness and let it shine out to the world like you know you can.

You've Got To Really Want It

When you really want your goal or Priceless Life Destination and I mean really want it, you'll kick start an internal booster system inside that will become so intense and hungry that it will smash through anything that stands in your way. You'll start by catching yourself saying *"I'll show you, there's always more than one way to skin a cat"* you'll find that nothing gets in your way and once something does and you conquer it you will have built up evidence and brand new references inside your subconscious mind to tell you if this happens again then I got over it last time and I will again.

You start to build up inner strength and confidence based in your past attempts when you smashed through a barrier that held you back previously.

Just thinking about your goal makes you feel good, because when you focus on what you really want and think about it you start to smile. So everyday think about what it is you want. What is it that you want to achieve and I promise it will make you feel good, practise that feeling of feeling good about yourself everyday. Let me ask you a question *"could you give me one good reason why you wouldn't do this?"*

Get into the habit of setting goals for yourself each day, get yourself in the zone each day so you're always thinking about always focusing on your Priceless Life Destination. Tune in with that satellite navigation system and that success seeking missile and you will, just like a magnet start to attract all the things into your life that you need to achieve your dreams.

Open The Door To Endless Possibilities.

- Imagine you have been born with that secret ingredient to attain anything you desire

- Take time out to have a look at what and how your own personal thinking has created your own world.
- Ask yourself this question, what could I change about the way I think?
- What do I think about, talk about. What do I want and what don't I want.
- Is it worth the effort?
- If there was one simple action I could do right now as a result of the answers above what would it be?

Remember we all see the world through our own eyes and place a certain amount of significance on certain areas of our lives. Our own perception is our own reality, no ones reality is the same.

The best way to know where you're going is to set yourself a goal. I know, I know you've heard it before but without a clear precise goal of what you want to achieve, how will you know when you've made it, how will you know when you've got there. Always remember if you don't set a target for what you want you'll hit your target every time. Anyone can hit nothing it's easy.

An awesome exercise I take my clients through when it comes to goal setting, is firstly to take a second to clear your mind free of any preconceived notions you currently have, now I know you have them, we all have them if you didn't you'd already be at your goal now, right! It's normal to have fears and doubts however these fears, doubts or even lack of confidence can be useful & there's always reasons why they exist which we'll come to soon.

So clear your mind and ask yourself this question what would my priceless life destination look like? What would I really love to achieve? What goal would I love to attain? Go on get clear and specific, it can't just be I want to earn more money or be financially free or be fitter, it's a great way to start but go much deeper inside.

It's Really Important To Set Goals For All different Areas Of Our Lives.

I want you to set your goals or your priceless life destinations for all different areas of your life, you'll be able to write them down in the spaces I've prepared for you in the next few pages, in your Priceless Life Destination Action Plan. At the moment we are just going to run through what you're going to do and how you're going to do it.

These are the areas of your life I want you to set goals for.

- Personal Goals (Health, Love, Quality of Life, Self Awareness or Growth, Set Up Your Own Business, Change Your Career.)
- Stuff You'd Love To Own Goals (Cars, Houses, etc.)
- Financial Goals (How much money you want to earn or save etc.)

You'll know what's right for you, just write it down and write down as many as possible

"REMEMBER if you don't write it down your life wont change."

This Is Important

When you're doing this exercise you must not be disturbed, turn off your phone, make sure the kids are fast asleep, this requires your full attention, no interruptions at all, this is IMPORTANT, this is your life. If you want your life to get better and have what you want, then this must be done correctly.

Some people find to get into the flow of knowing what they want, it's easier to record it first and then write it down, you'll know which way is best for you. (You can easily record it on your phone these days it's that easy.) But remember it's so important to write it down afterwards don't just leave it on your phone forever or you won't get it done. You must commit to writing it down, or what I call *"think in ink."* As only when you write it down does it become real as it causes a neurological pathway from the pen and paper to your brain which sets the wheels and cogs in motion. Then and only then will you start to attract these things into your life.

Don't worry or think of how you're going to do it just get it down on the Priceless Life Destination Action Planner for now.

The Next Principle

Remember I'm Just Explaining What We're doing, So You'll Get An Idea Of What We're going To Do. You'll Do It In The Next Section.

Set A Deadline For Each Goal

Why is this important?

If you don't set a time limit on your goals you'll do what you've always done and just stroll through life never completing anything. What happens with your tax return there's a set date to complete it by and if you don't you have to pay penalties. This is exactly how you want to set your goals. You MUST have a set deadline date to achieve your goals by. If you don't then you will pay the penalty of not having, being or doing what you want.

Look at your Priceless Life Destinations or goals and set a deadline for each goal. A date when you want to achieve it by. Even if you don't know how to achieve it, don't worry we'll get to that later lets just get it down on paper first.

Set deadlines like this, things you can achieve in:

- 1 Month.
- 2 Month.
- 3 Months.
- 6 Months.
- 1 Year.
- 2 Years.
- 3 Years.
- 4 Years.
- 5 Years.

Some deadlines could be short and others could be a few years, you'll know what's right for you and your Priceless Life and by how much time, effort and commitment you're willing to put into it.

CHAPTER TWO

Why Oh Why Oh Why

Success is the ability to go from one failure to another with no loss of enthusiasm

Winston Churchill.

The exercise I use with my clients is *"why do you want that"*. So for example, let's say you want to set up your own business.

Why do you want that?

Let's say your answer is being my own boss will allow me to earn more money and I wont have a boss to answer to.

"Great, why do you want that?"

The why or the reason you want it is the motivating factor so you can achieve what you want, but and this is a big but you must have enough reasons or enough why's or you'll just go back to what you did before and wont be bothered in achieving your priceless life destination

You have to come up with enough why's or reasons because the why's or reasons always have an emotion behind them, as human beings we do things due to emotional responses and connections that we have linked between our conscious and subconscious mind and it's that emotion or the way that we feel that creates the motion, to keep you constantly moving forward towards your priceless life. All of our behaviours are emotionally driven so we must get in to the habit of finding that emotion to create the motion to release the motivating factor to get where you need to get much quicker.

Keep asking yourself *"why do I want that"* until you feel an unfamiliar emotion or feeling of when it's just right for you.

How will you know when you cracked it and you've got the right answer, you'll know my friend because it will just feel right for you. How do we know when were in love? We just know right. This is just the same you'll just know, getting the right answer for you here is really important. Remember our perception is our reality.

Let's Start By Working Step by Step on Your Priceless Life

Again we need to *"think in ink"* write it down and the following charts will help you to set it into action for you.

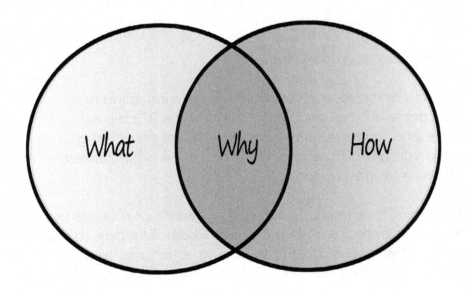

The chart shows how we make decisions in our lives and our thought process goes something like this. Ok I've got this goal that I need to achieve that's your what. Then you say to yourself how long will it take and how much of a pain or inconvenience will it cause me? That's your how. Now this is the key part, often too many people spend all their time or talking to themselves in the, what and the how of the process. They don't spend enough time in the in why of the process.

Remember the why or your reason is the foundation, the platform and the pillars of the whole asking process to success. The reason is because I think as we get older and we enter adult life, we find that life conditions us to stop asking the why questions. And the reason behind this is when you were younger and you didn't know the answer to a question at school and you wanted to ask why you didn't get it or just didn't understand it. This can make you feel like a bit of an idiot. Because you've got to put your hand up in front of the whole class so all your class mates know, you don't know the answer and it makes you feel like a bit stupid.

So as we get older we become conditioned not to ask why, so we don't look or feel like an idiot and this is what stops you. We have to right this situation now.

Start thinking like a small child again before the conditioning took over and start asking for the "_whys._" How many times for those of you who have children, do really young children constantly ask why when you tell them to do something. "Go and put your coat on" "_why_" "Were going out to the shops" "_why_" young children constantly ask why, they are always learning and soaking up stuff like a sponge

It's our "_why's_" or enough reasons of why we want to obtain the goal, the things that it will do for us on a positive basis that will make us follow through on the goal and obtain it. Because if you haven't got enough reasons of why you want this goal then you'll do what you've always done and it will just be a wishy washy dream.

We make our decisions down to our emotions and it's our emotions that cause the motion for us to take action. So we all make our decisions in life which according to our emotions which are our feelings. In fact scientific tests have proven that 95% of our decisions that we make in life, we make emotionally.

Let's say you want to buy a new car or house, to buy this new house or car you will have to put down more of a deposit. You'll also have to increase your monthly payments. Do we buy that car or that house on a logical decision, or an emotional decision? Of course we buy it emotionally, it doesn't make sense to increase your monthly payments and take money from your savings to fund it does it?

The left side of our brain deals in logic and the right hand side of our brain deals in emotions. So remember it's the emotion that creates the motion to get people to take action, just like all the emotional reasons you made up of why increasing your mortgage payments or your car payments was a good idea. You must come up with enough reasons or enough <u>why's</u> for you to really want your new priceless life destination or goal.

We all make our decisions with our emotions but then we justify our emotional decisions with logic. We do the same when we go on holiday; you go to the travel agents and the travel agent tells you all about the great hotel, the sun, the beach and the great food, as human beings we see ourselves sitting by the pool drinking margaritas, looking great with a tan, we really get a feel for it and how wonderful it's going to be, don't We? Then what happens, when we get home we look at the brochure to justify or rationalise the decision we've just made, of why we spent so much money.

Afterwards we look at it logically and say to ourselves *"I need a holiday and this is just right for me." "Without a holiday I'd just overload, I need time to relax and unwind."* Then you say to yourself, *"Well it sounded and felt good when I booked the holiday and now I better go and study the details of it".* Then you talk to yourself and reassure yourself of <u>why</u> it's such a good idea to spend all that money for just two weeks. I'm sure we've all done that at one time in our lives before haven't we?

When you get in touch with your <u>*"why"*</u>, which are your passion and your deep driving desire for what you want, something quite magical happens. When you are really clear on your <u>*"why"*</u> it becomes connected with your subconscious as you dream. As you become connected to your subconscious as you dream, you begin to access your emotions which are involved in your <u>*"why."*</u> By pure magic you'll begin to receive the <u>*"how's"*</u> for new resources and connections and new ideas that will transform your dream into a reality.

CHAPTER THREE

The Invisible Giant

As humans we don't make decisions in our lives based on what we know, we make decisions in our own lives based on how it will make us feel now and in the future.

Craig Price

Far too many people in life give up way too quickly. The average person gives up after trying something just once. The other people give up before they even try, that's why there are not many successful people in the world.

One of the main reasons people give up so quickly or don't even give it a go, is because we all have invisible barriers or mental road blocks that stop us. As soon as we set ourselves a goal we hit a road block or a barrier or brick wall of some sort that just stops us dead in our tracks.

I believe that each and every one of us has unlimited potential inside us, just waiting to shine out to share with the world. However we don't let it shine because of mental barriers that we install and these barriers stop us attaining our dreams.

These barriers kill our dreams, these barriers control our lives and these barriers control our habits, routines, actions and our behaviours. But more importantly these barriers control our thinking and the way we feel. As humans we don't make decisions in our lives based on what we know, we make decisions in our lives based on how it makes us feel.

If we feel these barriers will bring pain, fear, doubt, worry, anxiety and disruption into our lives, we just won't do it. These barriers must be addressed now for you to attain greatness in your life.

Did you know that it is a well known fact that the most successful people on the planet have failed way more times than they have succeeded? Successful people try more things than the average person and if they encounter failure. They don't dwell in self pity thinking and saying to themselves *"I knew this was going to happen."* They get up and try and try again.

It's a part of life that you should expect to fail many, many times before you succeed. You should look upon failure as a lesson learned in the ongoing road and process of becoming successful. Failing is part of the price and the inconvenience you must pay, see it as the paving stones on your road to success. Each paving stone you've trod on along your pathway is a learning curve to your own individual greatness.

Finding those barriers that hold you back are the key to your ongoing success. Always ask *"What is it that's holding me back?"* or *"what is it that keeps stopping me all the time?"* Constantly investigate and identify all of those barriers and road blocks and brick walls that are between you and your Priceless Life Destination.

There's Always A Solution To Every Problem

If there wasn't a solution to every problem we wouldn't have been able to go to the moon, or even fly in aeroplanes would we?

Remember you become what you think about most of the time. If you are constantly thinking about your difficulties you'll never see the wood for the trees. If you constantly focus on what you don't want, you'll never find a solution. However if you are always looking for a solution to your problems, (or what I like to call them challenges) you'll find a solution because your subconscious mind will be on the lookout for it for you.

When you constantly look for solutions in your life, you'll find ways of going through, over, under or around your barriers. Write down absolutely everything that you can think of that's standing in your way, or blocking you or stopping or slowing you down or just causing you an inconvenience from achieving your Priceless Life Destination.

People who dwell on their problems tell everyone how bad their life is, they want to share it with everyone and continue to complain all the time. They blame their lives on people and circumstances. They tell people how unhappy they are and how angry they feel about it.

Successful people do something completely different, they are constantly working on solutions and are always looking for solutions and simply say *"Right I've got this challenge, how can I solve it?"* Then they take action on their solutions and deal with the problem instantly, because they know if they don't do it instantly then tomorrow never comes.

There will always be problems in your life, this is why so often success is referred to as the ability to solve problems. Just like everything else in life it's a skill anyone can learn. The quicker you become at solving your problems, the quicker you'll get at solving the next problem. People often say the more successful I become the bigger my problems seem to be. It's a fact that the better you get at solving your problems; just like a magnet you'll attract even more into your life. Remember life is all about solving problems.

Each and every single person has the talent and ability to solve any barrier that's has been stopping them. But you must want that goal so much, that you can only think of its achievement and not of its limiting control or restrictions or excuse that have previously held you its hostage. Only when you can do this will you be able to move quickly towards your dreams.

Focus on those restrictions and limiting controls which you have allowed to steal your dreams. In the chart you'll see what I mean. The two main barriers can be fear and doubt. This is because as soon as people think of a new goal all that fear bubbles up inside and it takes over their lives and stops them instantly in their tracks. I have so many clients who want to start their own business, but that fear of actually doing it stops them dead in their tracks and kills their dreams instantly.

Doubt is very similar to fear for most people, as it works on our feelings. People seem to hang on to a conviction or an idea that they are inferior, or are not good enough or lack some magic ingredient that other people possess. Just like most things in life, fear and doubt are learned behaviours and if you can learn something you can unlearn it. To do this you do it in exactly the same way as you learned it, by practising and repetition.

Below Is What Often Happens When You Set Your-self A Goal

Below is what happens when successful people set a goal

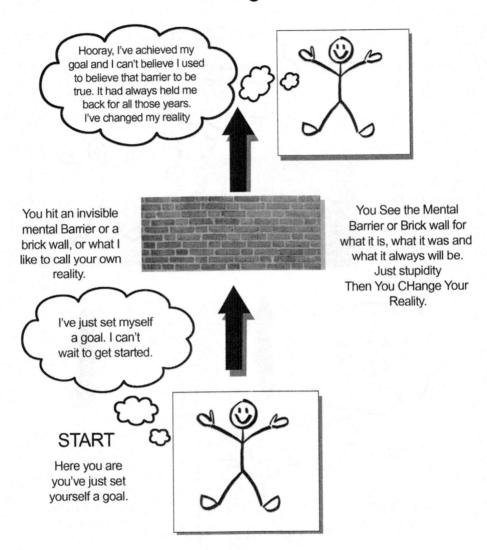

Remember we're not doing it yet I'm just explaining to you how we are going to do it, you'll do it on the next few pages on your Priceless Life Destination Action Plan

This is the secret formula right now, this is why every time before if you've set a goal for yourself and it hasn't worked. If you don't do this step right NOW for your priceless life destinations, I promise you it won't work and you'll always continue to do what you've always done before, never followed through on your goals. Remember if you do what you've always done you'll always get the same results guaranteed.

So here it is, I want you to imagine or think about or get a sense or a feeling, that you are working on one of your goals on your priceless life destination List. Close your eyes see it in full colour, hear it in full surround sound, see, feel, hear and see yourself starting to work towards your priceless life right now.

As you're doing this, I want you to notice what comes to mind, what are you thinking about what's stopping you?

Let me show you how some of the negative thoughts we have, fears and doubts can be useful and there's always a reason why they exist.

Brains think negatively because negativity is the way our brain protects us from harm. We have fears and doubts because it's our brains way of saying, hang on a minute something's not quite right here, something could get me in danger. In fact tests have shown that up to 80% of our thoughts at any given time are negative. This is what I call the Triple D Dragon and we'll cover this later on in the book.

Feel all the feelings that you associate with these mental road blocks or invisible barriers we all have, think of all the things that have stopped you in the past before. Think of all the things that have been blocking you attaining your goal or priceless life before. Think of all the things you've said to yourself on a regular basis and just experience the feelings and sensations, what comes up for you?

Some people feel pain; some people feel anger or doubt, fear, disappointment a sense of loss or even impossibility. You'll probably find tons and tons of excuses that crop up, or start coming to mind right now. You may even find it's certain people or circumstances or even certain events or stories you've told yourself over the years. These are the things that have stopped you and your priceless life being your reality.

Now write it all down, write all of it down, and don't leave anything out !!!!!

When you've finished writing everything down that you can think of, you'll probably have a list similar to this:

- I feel like I don't have the right education
- I feel like I'm not confident enough
- I feel like I'm not good enough
- I feel like I'm too young
- I feel like I'm too old
- I feel like I can't be bothered
- I feel like it's going to be hard work

Notice that the above list is all about how you feel, there's no follow on sentence because it's just a statement, it just is, it's the way that "I" feel and that's the way it is. The way we feel massively affects the way we see the world, if we don't feel confident will we ever get the job done? Of course we won't. If we don't feel smart enough or if we've not attained the right education will we ever follow through on our goals? Of course we won't.

The Next Step, The Secret Step

The way we feel massively affects our lives. I now want you to feel all the feelings you associate, with all the reasons you've just listed above. This is an easy exercise that I do with my clients and this is the secret ingredient that makes all the difference.

Visualise or imagine yourself whichever is easier for you *(some people like to close their eyes you'll know what's best for you)* working on one of your priceless life destinations. Fully associate with all the feelings of why you've not achieved it in the past, with the list you've just written down. Notice where those feelings are inside your body, some people feel it as a pain in the chest whilst other people feel it as an anger in their stomach and some people find it's a nervousness or anxiousness in their breathing or the way they hold themselves, whatever is right for you, you'll just instinctively know.

Allow yourself full permission to let all of those feelings, emotions or internal representations to do what they've always done in the past. Allow them to fully appear and come up and notice what they feel like and where they are in your body.

Now remember these feelings, where are they in your body where do they start and where do they finish, where do they give you the most discomfort and what does it feel like, feeling like this. I know this bit is the painful bit, but we've got to get through this if you want your own priceless life to happen for you.

Now write all of those feelings down on your Priceless Life Destination Action Plan. Because it's these feelings that have always stopped you, it's these feelings that have always cost you; it's these feelings that have held your happiness and your priceless life hostage for all these years.

The Next Step

Ask yourself a great question; remember when you ask yourself a great question you'll come up with a great answer

Here are the questions to ask:

1. Why do I keep doing that?
2. Why do I believe that to be true?
3. Is it really true? Or is it something I've just taken on board years ago and kept it locked away in the corridor of doorways in my subconscious mind. Which over time has made me think, feel, act and behave in a certain way for all these years.

Answer those three questions fully and honestly just like I did, in the introduction of this book when the day my life changed. That was the day when I actually caught myself doing it, when I sat in the industrial estate doing what I'd always done to myself before. Constantly arguing for my limitations all day long and the crazy thing was, I didn't even know I was doing it.

The reason I didn't even know I was doing it, was because I believed it to be true and when you believe something to be true, you very rarely question it. The reason is simply because you've locked it away in that corridor of doorways, inside your subconscious mind for all those years and you have built up enough evidence and references of why you believe it to be true. Our subconscious minds being the wonderful tool it is, only acts out and plays out our most dominating thoughts as that becomes our own reality.

Remember the questions I asked myself *"why is it, I can knock on that company door but I can't knock on this one"* my answer was because *"I don't feel confident enough"* my second question was *"why is it I don't feel confident enough"* my answer was *"because that's a big company and big companies don't do business with small companies"*

My next question was "*is that true, do big companies do business with little companies*" and my answer was "*yes they do, so if they do I can't believe that to be true anymore. Because only an idiot would believe that to be true*" and then just take five minutes and let that thought process go. It's easy to do because you don't believe it to be true anymore.

Then ask yourself "*where on earth did that belief system come from*" and the only thing I could have thought where it came from, was someone years ago must have told me that, they or a friend of there's tried to do business with a big business and failed. So in other words, their own belief system was passed onto me and I believed it.

I see other people's opinions, belief systems and points of view a bit like smelly farts. They come out just when you don't want them to and they stink up your head.

After you've gone through this process and you've now realised that for all these years you've believed in something that just wasn't true. Simply take five minutes and see it for what it was, see it for what it is and see it for what it always will be, just stupidity. Laugh at it and I mean laugh out loud, because you cannot believe it to be true anymore and it was just a silly thing to believe anyway wasn't it?

The next step is to think about your goal or priceless life destination but this time, with your new eyes of seeing the world. Now you've realised that it's not true anymore, that mental blocker can no longer be there. If the blocker isn't there, neither can the feelings that you associated with it and you'll now notice they have also gone.

Remember where the feeling was in your body before, when you had the invisible roadblock or mental barrier and try and think about what used to hold you back. You'll find you no longer have the same feelings or internal representation inside your body. This is because you can no longer believe in anything that isn't true, only an idiot would believe in something that wasn't true and as you're an intelligent person, you can no longer believe it to be true anymore. Can you?

You'll find the crazy thing is, the more you try to think about it, the more if feels like it isn't even you and you can't believe that you once used to do that, or even used to believe that was true. You have now changed your reality and you are seeing the world differently.

"Congratulations, you've just broken down, destroyed and eliminated a mental road block or invisible barrier."

The Next Step

Take massive action towards your priceless life *right NOW…*

It doesn't matter what you do as long as it's taking action towards your priceless life, the secret is to do it now. Maybe it's enrolling onto a university or college course or joining a gym or make that life changing phone call.

Action is the key and the best way to start taking action is to start by doing the small stuff first. Have you ever been watching your favourite television programme before and you've wanted to go to the toilet for a wee, I'm sure this has happened to you hundreds of times before.

Well what happens, do you go to the toilet immediately? No of course you don't you sit there and say to yourself *"I'll go when the advert break comes on."* Now when the advert break comes do you then go to the toilet? NO you then say to yourself *"I'll wait until the next advert break and I'll go then."*

If you can't get enough motivation to get up immediately and go to the toilet and not wet yourself, how are you going to start taking action straight away on your priceless life? You must work on the small things first, get into habits of doing things immediately.

Catch yourself when you put things off, this is called procrastination, always putting things off till tomorrow. When the bin is full at home don't just place more rubbish inside it and do the balancing act until everything is falling out and it eventually makes a mess all over the floor. Get into a habit and a routine and empty the bin immediately. Remember we are what we repeatedly do and if you keep putting things off till tomorrow you'll never attain your priceless life. Get into the habit of doing the small stuff around the house and soon enough, it will become second nature and you'll start taking action immediately on your priceless life.

I believe your mind is like a corridor of locked doorways and behind each doorway is a disempowering belief system. What is a disempowering belief? It's something negative that you believe to be true, that you've held onto for years. Let me explain, it's a bit like a young boy talking to his Dad and saying *"dad I want to be a millionaire"* and his dad says to him *"don't be silly son, nobody from our family has ever become a millionaire so it's not going to happen for you. Just set your sights a bit lower so you won't be disappointed and don't forget you come from Manchester and there's not that many millionaires around here."* As human beings we say the following to ourselves. *"My dad says this will never happen to me, I must really set my sights lower and because I live in Manchester I won't become a millionaire."* Now the truth of the matter is this. Someone's son or daughter will become a millionaire, regardless of where they live or what family they've been born into, wont they?

As human beings our mind makes up all types of reasons excuses based on the things we believe to be true *(which is our own reality)* so we don't act on our life and have all the things we want or become the person we so desperately want to be.

Let me ask you a question. Who tells you if something is good or bad? You do, don't you? You are the master of your own reality. Your own individual reality is based on your previous experiences and references that you've had in the past. Your reality is perceived by how you thought something was good or bad for you in the past. You automatically made up your mind with that style of reasoning based on your past experiences. Remember that other people's opinions are very powerful and they can also make you believe in things that quite simply aren't true.

Success Summary

Action Steps To Take for Completing
Your Priceless Life Destination Action Plan

- Ask for what you want.
- Be really specific on what you want in every area of your life.
- Write your goals down *"Think In Ink"*
- Set a start date and a finish date to your goals.
- Ask yourself *"why do I really want it."*
- Ask yourself *"what's been stopping me from reaching my goals before."* And imagine yourself working towards your goals.
- Feel all the feelings that you associate inside your body, remember where they are inside your body and what they do and where they move to. Then write them down.
- Ask yourself the following
- *"Why do I keep doing that"*
- *"Why do I believe it to be true"*
- Once you've found the reason or belief system, question it until you don't believe it to be true anymore.

- Think about your goal again and notice how differently you feel, now that you don't believe it to be true anymore.

We've talked about it enough; it's time to start creating your new life and the new you. Fill in your Priceless Life Destination Action Plan.

Do you know the Number 1 secret of highly successful people? They dream **BIG** dreams.

Marcus Aurelius said, *"Dream big dreams, only big dreams have the power to move men's souls."*

Donald Trump said, *"As long as you are going to dream, dream big."*

Take your dreams and turn them into goals.

Many people are afraid of setting goals because they are afraid of not reaching them. Do you know that only 3% of people in the world have clearly defined written goals? Did you also know that they earn 10 times more than the other 97% combined?

Let my words motivate and inspire you to achieve your greatest desires; we become what we think about and dream about. It is impossible for us to bring success, happiness and wealth into our lives if we are constantly thinking about failure and poverty. If you are not experiencing the life that you want, start dreaming now.

Start dreaming about your business, your relationships and your future again.

Don't allow your present situation to become your future destination. Start living and experiencing a life worth living, your success depends on it. You have the power to change the course of your future forever, *"DO IT NOW."*

Below is your Priceless Life Destination Action Plan for all areas of your life. You now have a choice, you can either sit back and continue to do what you've always done and your life won't change, or you can chose to do it now. Make the right decision and learn what thousands of others have, my principles just work. But you've got to take action on them, to make them work. *"TAKE ACTION NOW."*

Priceless Life Destination Action Plan

Personal Goals

Remember think in ink,
if you don't write this down
your life wont change

Personal Goals (Health, Love, Quality of Life, Self Awareness or Growth, Set Up Your Own Business. You can either write them all down below or just one and re print the sheet each time)

_____

_____

_____

_____

_____

_____

_____

_____

_____

_____

_____

_____

_____

_____

Give Your Goal A Name (So when talking to yourself, you'll easily be able to refer to it)

_____

_____

_____

Date You Set Your Goal.

_____

_____

Date You Want To Achieve The Goal By.

_____

_____

Why Do I Want This Goal? (What will you get personally by achieving this goal? Remember the "_why_" is your motivating factor. Write down each reason or why.)

_____

_____

_____

_____

_____

_____

_____

_____

_____

_____

_____

_____

Write Down All The Stuff That's In Your Way. (All that stuff you used to do, all the things, the excuses in your way that stopped you achieving your goal before. Or the story you always told yourself.)

_____

_____

_____

_____

_____

_____

_____

_____

_____

_____

_____

_____

_____

_____

Associate With The Feelings Inside Your Body That You Have Towards Your Goal. (Where in your body are these mental road-blocks & invisible barriers, what do they do, what do they feel like & where do they move to.)

_____

_____

_____

_____

_____

_____

_____

_____

_____

_____
_____
_____
_____
_____

Ask Yourself The Following:

Why Do I Keep Doing That?

_____
_____
_____
_____
_____

Why Do I Believe It To Be True?

_____
_____
_____
_____
_____
_____

Is It Really True? (Or just something or someone else's opinion I took on board years ago and kept it locked away in the corridor of doorways in my subconscious mind. That has made me think, feel, act and behave in a certain way for all these years.)

_____
_____
_____
_____

Associate Again With The Feelings Inside Your Body That You Have Towards Your Goal & Notice All The Differences Now That You Don't Believe It To Be True Anymore. (Now you've seen it for what it is, what it was and what it always will be just stupidity and it's not true laugh at it. Your world is now full of opportunities. Write down below what new exciting feelings you are experiencing inside your body and where they are and what new actions you are going to take.)

New Exciting Feelings

Action Number 1.

_____
_____
_____
_____
_____
_____
_____

Action Number 2.

_____
_____
_____
_____
_____
_____
_____

Action Number 3.

_____
_____
_____
_____
_____
_____
_____

Priceless Life Destination Action Plan

Stuff &Things Goals
(Cars, Houses, Clothes, Jewellery)

Remember think in ink,
if you don't write this down
your life wont change

Stuff & Things Goals (what car do you want to drive, what house do you want to own & what clothes or jewellery do you want to own or wear.)

_____

_____

_____

_____

_____

_____

_____

_____

_____

_____

_____

_____

_____

_____

_____

Give Your Goal A Name (So when talking to yourself, you'll easily be able to refer to it)

_____

_____

_____

Date You Set Your Goal.

_____

_____

Date You Want To Achieve The Goal By.

_____

_____

Why Do I Want This Goal? (What will you get personally by achieving this goal? Remember the "_why_" is your motivating factor. Write down each reason or why.)

_____

_____

_____

_____

_____

_____

_____

_____

_____

_____

_____

_____

Write Down All The Stuff That's In Your Way. (All that stuff you used to do, all the things, the excuses in your way that stopped you achieving your goal before. Or the story you always told yourself.)

_____

_____

_____
_____
_____
_____
_____
_____
_____
_____
_____
_____
_____
_____
_____
_____
_____
_____
_____

Associate With The Feelings Inside Your Body That You Have Towards Your Goal. (Where in your body are these mental roadblocks & invisible barriers, what do they do, what do they feel like & where do they move to.)

_____
_____
_____
_____
_____
_____
_____
_____
_____
_____
_____
_____
_____
_____

Ask Yourself The Following:

Why Do I Keep Doing That?

_____

_____

_____

_____

_____

Why Do I Believe It To Be True?

_____

_____

_____

_____

_____

Is It Really True? (Or just something or someone else's opinion I took on board years ago and kept it locked away in the corridor of doorways in my subconscious mind. That has made me think, feel, act and behave in a certain way for all these years.)

_____

_____

_____

_____

Associate Again With The Feelings Inside Your Body That You Have Towards Your Goal & Notice All The Differences Now That You Don't Believe It To Be True Anymore. (Now you've seen it for what it is, what it was and what it always will be just stupidity and it's not true, laugh at it. Your world is now full of opportunities. Write down below what new exciting feeling you are experiencing inside your body and where they are and what new actions you are going to take.)

New Exciting Feelings

_____

_____

_____

_____

_____

_____

_____

_____

_____

_____

_____

_____

_____

Action Number 1.

_____

_____

_____

_____

_____

_____

_____

Action Number 2.

_____

_____

_____

_____

_____

_____

_____

Action Number 3.

_____

_____

_____

_____

_____

_____

_____

Priceless Life Destination Action Plan

Financial Goals
(How Much You Want To Earn & Save)

Remember think in ink,
if you don't write this down
your life wont change

Financial Goals (How much money do you want to earn or save)

_____
_____
_____
_____
_____
_____
_____
_____
_____
_____
_____
_____
_____
_____

Give Your Goal A Name (So when talking to yourself, you'll easily be able to refer to it)

_____
_____
_____

Date You Set Your Goal.

_____
_____

Date You Want To Achieve The Goal By.

_____
_____

Why Do I Want This Goal? (What will you get personally by achieving this goal? Remember the "_why_" is your motivating factor. Write down each reason or why.)

_____
_____
_____
_____
_____
_____
_____
_____
_____
_____
_____
_____

Write Down All The Stuff That's In Your Way. (All that stuff you used to do, all the things, the excuses in your way that stopped you achieving your goal before. Or the story you always told yourself.)

_____
_____
_____

———————————————
———————————————
———————————————
———————————————
———————————————
———————————————
———————————————
———————————————
———————————————
———————————————
———————————————
———————————————

Associate With The Feelings Inside Your Body That You Have Towards Your Goal. (Where in your body are these mental road-blocks & invisible barriers, what do they do, what do they feel like & where do they move to.)

———————————————
———————————————
———————————————
———————————————
———————————————
———————————————
———————————————
———————————————
———————————————
———————————————
———————————————
———————————————

Ask Yourself The Following:

Why Do I Keep Doing That?

_____

_____

_____

_____

_____

Why Do I Believe It To Be True?

_____

_____

_____

_____

_____

Is It Really True? (Or just something or someone else's opinion I took on board years ago and kept it locked away in the corridor of doorways in my subconscious mind. That has made me think, feel, act and behave in a certain way for all these years.)

_____

_____

_____

_____

Associate Again With The Feelings Inside Your Body That You Have Towards Your Goal & Notice All The Differences Now That You Don't Believe It To Be True Anymore. (Now you've seen it for what it is, what it was and what it always will be just stupidity and it's not true, laugh at it. Your world is now full of opportunities. Write down below what new exciting feeling you are experiencing inside your body and where they are and what new actions you are going to take.)

New Exciting Feelings

_____

_____

_____

_____

_____

_____

_____

_____

_____

_____

_____

_____

Action Number 1.

_____

_____

_____

_____

_____

_____

_____

Action Number 2.

_____

_____

_____

_____

_____

_____

_____

Action Number 3.

_____

_____

_____

_____

_____

_____

_____

Follow These Next Principles For All Areas Of Your Goals

Look in to The Future and Imagine You Didn't Achieve Your Goal. With that disappointed feeling in mind, ask yourself this question. If only I would of done........................ Then I would of reached my goal (Now fill in the missing area below.)

_____
_____
_____
_____
_____
_____
_____
_____
_____

Now You Know The Reasons In The Past, Why You've Always Failed In Reaching Your Goals Before. (Write down all the new empowering actions or solutions you are going to do now, to stop it happening again.)

_____
_____
_____
_____
_____
_____
_____
_____

Rewarding Yourself (What reward or treat will you give yourself when you've achieved it or are half way there or even part way there. It is so important to reward yourself when you start working towards your goal, it keeps you motivated & on track.)

1. Achieved The Goal.

_____

_____

_____

_____

2. Half Way To Your Goal.

_____

_____

_____

_____

3. Part Way To Your Goal.

_____

_____

_____

_____

Now Write A Sentence Below

Final Goal (Begin goal statement with "I'm so happy and grateful now that..." state goal in present tense: "I am.." "I have...", etc. and must include date goal will be achieved)

_____

_____

_____

_____

_____

_____

_____

_____

_____

_____

_____

_____

_____

_____

_____

_____

_____

_____

_____

CHAPTER FOUR

Take Control Of Your Remote Control

If you don't push the right buttons in your life, society, friends, family and circumstances will push them for you.

Craig Price

Fifteen years ago I was struggling in my business. I was in to my overdraft by almost £12,000 due to a company I did business with going into receivership. So if you're reading this and you've got £5 in your wallet you've got more money than I had when I first started my journey.

I couldn't afford to do the nice things I wanted to do, or go to the places I wanted to go. I was stuck in a perpetual Monday morning blaming everything and everyone for my results in life.

One day I had what they call an epiphany, it totally changed and transformed my life. I suddenly became aware that everything that was going to happen to me in the future was up to me and if I didn't change straight away then I was doomed for failure. I knew that if things were going to get better it would have to begin with me. If I didn't make the necessary changes in my life then I would be destined for doom and mediocrity. It was my responsibility to change no one else, just mine.

You know when certain moments in your life just stick; well this is one of them for me. I had constantly been standing in my comfort zone always stuck right in the middle of it, waiting for that magic moment to come my way. Which surprise, surprise never did, I was thinking to myself come on, now is the time if I don't do it now that's it. I'll be a failure forever and never amount to anything.

I thought back to all the times when I was younger, dreaming about owning a Rolls Royce and a Mercedes Benz. I even used to park my car outside the Rolls Royce factory and watch them bring them outside thinking to myself "one day I'll have one." Where had all those dreams gone that I once had when I was younger, what had happened to all that potential I knew I had back then. I had let life take over and that new reality I had created for myself rule my world.

I quickly learnt that day, that when you accept totally complete responsibility for you and your life, it's as if you jump from childhood to adulthood in one step. However most people don't do this, I meet people everyday who are in their 60's and 70's who still argue for their limitations in their lives and blame their life on people, problems and circumstances. It's as if they are perpetually trapped in the past and can't seem to let go of it. They even get together with other people and love to tell each other how bad it's been for them they say things like *"if things were different then they would be different."* Or *" If only they were young now then all this wouldn't have happened as it's so much better for all of us now."*

The one thing that is common for all of us, is that life is full of problems all day, all week, every month and every year for each and every one of us. When you realise this you can move forward.

The biggest nemesis of attaining success is negative thinking and emotions, it's like a vampire it will drain all the energy out of you. A great goal to have is to free yourself from any negative thinking and emotions, the great news is this can be learnt. The nasty emotions of negativity, fear, procrastination, inferiority, jealousy, self pity and anger are caused by ourselves.

The day we remove these nasty patterns of behaviour from our lives the great feelings of happiness, excitement and enthusiasm will automatically run into our lives and change our lives for the better.

Push The Right Button & Control Your Emotions

If you want to stay positive stop criticising other people about their behaviours. Every single time you complain or argue or criticise someone else for something they have done or haven't done, guess what happens? You actually spark off feelings inside your body of negativity, anger or hatred and guess who is constantly suffering? That's right it's you. Your emotions of negativity or hatred don't affect the other person it only affects YOU.

When you allow yourself to be angry with someone or something you are allowing that person or that circumstance to take control of your remote control and push your buttons for you. Remember when we feel happiness and excitement we are nice to be around. When we're miserable, hostile and full of negativity do you know anyone that wants to hang out with us? No of course you don't, the only person who wants to be with you when you feel like this is you and you keep going over and over the same thing again and again.

The day that you decide to totally accept that you hold the remote control for the way that you think, feel, act and behave and for everything that happens to you, is 100% your responsibility. You will become the master of your Priceless Life Destination. In the next few chapters we will talk more about the way you think, feel act and behave later on in the book. I call it my T.F.A.B. Method.

It's Your Choice You Decide

You have controlled you and your life up to now, the choices and decisions you made last week, last month and last year, have got you to where you are today. If there's something you don't like in your life you are responsible for it. If you feel there's something you're not happy about or something you worry about it's up to you to change it and take and make the steps to improve your life.

You are 100% completely responsible for the way your life is today, and the results you've obtained and also the consequences of your actions and convictions. You are where you and who and what you are today because you've decided it to be that way. Whether you like it or not that is the truth.

In other words, have you often wondered why you always earn the same amount of money? It's because you've decided a base standard for what you want to earn, no more no less. If you're not currently happy with how much you earn each year, start right now and set that as a goal. Make a plan of what you'll need to do and start working on what you need to do, to earn what you really want to earn.

As the master of your remote control to you and your life you can create your own destiny, simply push the right buttons to set yourself free and make some new powerful decisions. Remember YOU are in charge of you and your Priceless Life Destination.

Push The Right Buttons To Take Control

Just as you are the master controller of your remote control for the way you think, feel, act and behave. You are the master controller of your own planning of your life and your career. You are the controller of your plans, your strategies, setting goals and setting a higher standard of living for yourself.

You are the controller for the quality and quantity of the work you do. You are the controller of the results you obtain and expect to get. You are also the controller of the self image you have, you are the controller of your how much money you want to earn. You are the controller of how much you want to save or invest; you are also the controller of who you have relationships with.

Be careful, you choose which buttons you push, your choice of buttons has a massive impact on how much you'll learn, how much you'll earn and how fast you'll get ahead and also how happy you'll be at home or in your career.

As the master controller of your remote control to your life, you are in complete control of what new skills you'll need to attain and continue to learn to become the new you. Remember no one is going to do it for you, you'll have to do that all by yourself. if you don't constantly learn new ideas and strategies in your life to help you create your new future, you'll still be the same old person doing the same old stuff. We all have to continuously learn or re learn new techniques if we want to grow.

See Yourself As The Master Of Your Vey Own Remote Control

From this point forward, see yourself as the true master of your destiny or Priceless Life Destination. You are 100% in charge of you and your own life. See yourself in charge of your very own remote control, instantly knowing exactly which button to push and when to push it. See yourself as that powerful, confident and self reliant person that just instinctively knows which button to push to obtain the correct result at the right time.

Truly understand that you'll eliminate complaining or making excuses by pushing the right buttons, knowing that any negative thought process you can change instantly by pushing the right buttons. Knowing that if something bad happened in the past you can't change it, but you can push new buttons to control your future. Know beyond a shadow of a doubt that you can move towards your new future. Automatically you'll consistently think about what you want and where you are going, just by pushing the right buttons on your remote control. Know that you have the right button at your command to think about your goals which makes you happy and powerful.

Holding Tightly Onto Your Remote Control.

Why is it some people feel completely in control of their lives and have confidence and have power and are optimistic about their future? While other people feel they have a lack of control in their lives and feel weak, fearful and have a sense they are controlled by the circumstances in their lives.

When you take full responsibility for yourself and your way of thinking and behaving and you start to admit that you are indeed the master of your very own remote control. Instantly you'll find yourself saying *"I am responsible for me and my future"* this will make you more confident and powerful and you'll start to develop in ways you previously thought was impossible.

Happiness and fulfilment work in exactly the same way. The more sense of responsibility you accept the greater amount of control you will have over your remote control of your experiences.

The more control you have and know you'll have, the more positive energy you will allow into your life. Really quickly you'll have the confidence, motivation, determination and inspiration to set new exciting and bigger goals for yourself. You'll instantly know that the remote control to your life is yours and it's now in your hands and you can make your life whatever you want it to look like.

Each Button Is At Your Command

You must have the feeling and realisation that you have at your fingertips, the unlimited power and potential to be, do and have anything you truly desire in life. If you're willing to work hard enough and long enough and you want it badly enough you will attain it.

Don't forget to accept complete 100% responsibility for you and your life and absolutely everything that happens to you, with no blaming other people or circumstances for you and your outcomes.

Once you have mastered these two principles and you are completely at the understanding of your unlimited potential you have inside. Then you are ready to move to the next principle which is to begin to design your very own Priceless Life Destination.

Push The Right Buttons Now, To Live Your Dreams

- Notice your biggest area of negativity in your life and discover what ways you're responsible for your situations in your life.
- Know beyond a shadow of a doubt that you hold the remote control to your life.
- In what ways would you act differently, now you know you hold the remote control to your life?
- Push the right buttons on you remote control and stop blaming anyone else and accept full responsibility in every area of your life.
- Stop making excuses all of the time and instead work towards your desired future, imagine you can push a button on your remote control to eliminate any excuses from your life.
- Know that you are where you are today because of the decisions you made in the past. Start thinking about what you should change right now.
- Push the let it go button, on your remote control. If anyone has ever hurt you in the past just let it go. Push the let it go button and don't allow yourself to talk about it ever again as it wastes too much precious time.

CHAPTER FIVE

See It As Done And Dusted

*The future belongs to those who believe
in the beauty of their dreams*

Eleanor Roosevelt

I've already said that we become what we think about, so what is it that successful people think about? It's simple, they only think and talk about the future and where they're going and what they've got to do to make it happen, to get there really quickly.

Guess what failures do? They only think about, only talk about the present moment or what problems they have. They continuously think and talk about what worries them now and what worried them in the past.

Successful people only think about only talk about, what they want and desire and where they want to go. They are always future orientated people. When you think about your future you begin to think like a successful person and you'll soon get the results they attain.

When you start to set yourself goals it's a great idea to set 5 year goals, think what your life would look like if it were perfect for you in every single way.

The biggest road block or invisible mental barrier to goal setting is your very own belief systems or your own reality. All of the reasons or a combination of evidence and references you've built up over the years of why you can't have your dream life.

You may well feel yourself to be inadequate in some way, or inferior in certain areas of your life. Such as intelligence, education, ability, talents or you may think you don't have a likeable personality. These self prophesising beliefs hold you and your happiness hostage and you either set no goals whatsoever, or you set goals so low that are truly below your own individual level of competency.

There's No Limits

When you start to practise future thinking, you actually cancel out the self limitation process. Just imagine right now there's no way and I mean no way that you could fail, in achieving one of your goals. Imagine you have everything you need all the attributes to succeed, imagine you have all the connections all the friends all the opportunities. Even all the luck you'll need and all the doorways of opportunity are wide open for you.

There are no limits or limitations on what you could be, or do or have. When you imagine the sky is the limit and you've reached your goal, ask yourself this simple question, *"what was it I did then that I'm not doing now, that got me to my goal?"*

You've then got the answer to your dreams and that's what you've got to do.

Never Say Never

When you practise future thinking you never say never with your dreams and visions for you and your future. You'll find that you will be attracted to big goals and big dreams rather than little goals. Constantly use forward and future thinking to just create your perfect future. Make your mind up on what you really want, then before you come back to the present moment deal with what you can in your current situation.

Start with your career. Take 5 minutes and think about what it would have to look like 5 years in the future, to be perfect for you.

Answer these questions.

- What would it look like?
- What would you be doing?
- Where would you be?
- What new skills and talents would you have?
- What new types of goals will you be achieving?

When you practise this type of thinking and have answered the above questions imagine you have no limits. Just imagine that everything and anything is possible for you.

When you start to do this, the only question that seems to always come up is how am I going to do it. Continuously ask it to yourself as it will release all the creativity inside your brain and will spark new ideas to attain your goals.

Remember failures always ask "*I wonder whether or not this goal is attainable or possible.*" Successful people only ever ask one question, "*how?*" Then they use everything in their capabilities to make their goals a reality.

As an avid fitness enthusiast, I couldn't make a blueprint for success and leave out health and fitness. Without your health you can't achieve any of your goals. You must make your health and fitness your utmost priority above everything else, and I mean above everything else. Don't just take your fitness for granted, whatever we eat today will become a part of our bodies in two weeks time.

If we eat a lamb chop and eat the fat of that chop the fat will become part of our bodies and will become part of our cellular structure. So we quite literally become what we eat, just like we become what we think about.

Health & Fitness

- If you were in awesome shape and had the body you would love to have five years from now, what would it look like?
- How heavy or light would you be?
- What would you look and feel like?
- How much exercise would you do each week?
- What new changes would you have to make in your diet and exercise routines to attain that awesome physique.

The Awesome Question

One of the greatest questions to ask yourself is:

"What do I really, really and I mean really, want to do with my life?"

If you could have anything, be anything or do anything what would it be? Remember that you really should return to this one question all the time over and over again in the months and years ahead.

When you first start setting goals, it can feel a bit weird. I know it did for me, it may even feel like a fantasy world or a bit dreamlike and not attached to reality. However now is the time to make them reality by following my Priceless Success Principles.

The Dreaded Comfort Zone

The comfort zone can be a huge challenge for most people, but if you don't overcome it you'll never achieve success. So many people become comfortable with their situations. They become comfortable with earning a particular level of income, they become comfortable with their current health and fitness levels. They become comfortable with their job or relationships. It's this level of comfort that stops and hinders them from making the specific changes in their lives for the better. It's as if their own individual comfort zone holds them responsible for making any changes at all.

Your own comfort zone is a huge roadblock or barrier to attaining your goals it kills determination, dedication and inspiration. People who get stuck in their own comfort zones can find it impossible to move forward in their life. You must find ways to jump out of your comfort zone. A great thing to remember is, even the most successful people in the world were at one time stuck in their comfort zone fearful of venturing out and attaining their goals.

Jumping Out Of Your Comfort Zone

The easiest way to jump out of your comfort zone and break free from that fear and levels of comfort, is to set yourself big challenging goals. Once you've set them break them up into small pieces or specific tasks, then set a deadline for each task and work on it every day.

Once you've broken it down into small tasks, organise each task by priority by writing it down, if you don't know which is the most important use your pen just like a magic wand and ask yourself *"by waving my magic wand and removing the most important task, so I could get to my goal much faster which one would it be?"* There's your answer.

Your own barriers or tasks that keep you in your comfort zone, are the things you must tackle immediately and set the appropriate steps to help remove them from your life. Remove them one at a time by prioritising them and simply use your magic wand or your pen to find out, which is the first one to remove.

You could even have a second goal list to remove the barriers, now that's food for thought. Just do exactly the same, give each barrier a deadline to remove it by.

The one trait all successful people have in common is they make a habit of doing things they don't like to do on a regular basis.

The Comfort Zone Rhyme

I used to have a comfort zone where I knew I wouldn't fail.
The same four walls and busywork were really more like jail.
I longed so much to do the things I'd never done before,
But stayed inside my comfort zone and paced the same old floor.

I said it didn't matter that I wasn't doing much.
I said I didn't care for things like commission cheques and such.
I claimed to be so busy with the things inside the zone,
but deep inside I longed for something special of my own.

I couldn't let my life go by just watching others win.
I held my breath; I stepped outside and let the change begin.
I took a step and with new strength I'd never felt before,
I kissed my comfort zone goodbye and closed and locked the door.

If you're in a comfort zone, afraid to venture out,
Remember that all winners were at one time filled with doubt.
A step or two and words of praise can make your dreams come true.
Reach for your future with a smile; success is there for you!

Author Unknown

CHAPTER SIX

The Dominating, Delusional, Destructive Dragon

Just like you protect your home from thieves, you must protect your life from your mind.
Or it will steal your life from under your nose.

Craig Price

What's the distance between success and failure?

It's easy; it's the 6 inches distance between ear to ear. What goes on in between your ears in your subconscious mind will determine how successful you become period.

When you can successfully control your mind or the voice or internal communication we all have with ourselves you will become successful.

As a man is what he thinks about all day long, whatever dominating thoughts you allow to control your subconscious mind, will become your very own individual reality.

Over the last 14 years, in my Psychotherapy and Life Coaching practise I have personally worked with thousands of patients who had suffered with fears, phobias, obsessions, addictions, panic & anxiety attacks & OCD's and repetitive and obsessive thoughts. I've helped clients who've always found themselves settling for a life of mediocrity, being stuck in the same old rut, never had self esteem or confidence, lacked motivation and dedication. Clients, who've found no matter what they did or how hard they worked, couldn't smash their barriers or mental roadblocks that have always held them back.

Over the years, people under my tutelage have made massive leaps in their ability to make money and produce extraordinary results in their lives. Live their life to the full and live free from any mental health challenge that once held them prisoner.

The results came because they worked on their inner greatness first, then applied that energy to their projects and goals. The secret ingredient was to control the Dominating, Delusional Destructive Dragon (The Triple D dragon) which is the nickname I use for your mind, that little voice inside your head.

I see the mind or that little voice that talks to you as a dragon. If you let a dragon loose in your house what would happen? It would cause chaos and carnage; it would destroy everything, wouldn't it. Well if you let your mind the Dominating Delusional Destructive Dragon (The Triple D Dragon) loose in your life then it will *DESTROY YOUR LIFE*

Let me ask you 2 questions:

- Do you talk to yourself, now if you're saying to yourself *"hmmm, do I talk to myself? I don't know I don't think so."* Then obviously you talk to yourself.
- Do you protect your home from thieves by closing your doors, installing burglar alarms and locking your windows? Of course you do, if you didn't then you would be asking for trouble wouldn't you?

Well the same goes for the Triple D Dragon if you don't protect yourself and your life from the Dominating Delusional Destructive Dragon (your mind) it will steal your life.

Most people achieve success hoping that they will finally be happy and fulfilled, only to be disappointed by the fact that they are now wealthy, but still the same person. It is who you are and your perspective on life that determines whether you are happy or not. So, let's start off with the how the Triple D Dragon works and controls your life.

Let Me Show You What The Dominating Delusional Destructive Dragon Has Already Done For You

We become what we think about on a regular basis; whatever dominating thoughts we allow to enter our own thoughts will become our own individual reality.

Let me ask you, have you ever:

Felt Fearful

Felt you weren't confident

Doubted you abilities

Worried about something or a circumstance in your life

Been concerned, that you're not good enough

Been concerned, you don't have the correct education

Worried about meeting new people

Procrastinated, put things off until tomorrow

Felt everyone else has good luck, while you don't

Believed that, you'll never have the success you've always wanted

Of course you have. We've all felt like this before, if you hadn't then you are simply not human, all of us at one time in our lives have felt these feelings.

This is the Triple D Dragon working his destructive patterns in your life; far too many of us worry ourselves throughout our lives trying to cope with things in our own little personal ways. Without controlling the Triple D Dragon, these things we all bring on ourselves through our own habitual way of thinking.

Everyone one of us are the sum total of our own thoughts, you are where you are in life today at this present moment because it's exactly where you really want to be. Even if you don't admit it to yourself, it's true. If you wanted better for yourself you would of done something about it, wouldn't you?

It's so important that we live off our own thoughts in the future and control our Dominating, Delusional, and Destructive Dragon. Because whatever you think about today, tomorrow, next week, next month and next year will mould your life and determine your Priceless Life Destination.

You are guided by your Triple D Dragon your mind.

You are where you are today because of your dominating thoughts that your dragon had yesterday, last week, last month and last year. You're sitting at the controls of your Triple D Dragon; you can either sit back and let it do what it's done for all of your life until this point right now. Or you can control and direct this awesome powerful beast and slay it. Then use its power to direct you to your Priceless Life Destination.

"It's up to YOU; YOU'RE IN CONTROL OF IT."

We must control our thinking.

The dragon that can bring us fear, procrastination, self doubt, worry and apprehension also has another nice side to him. This dragon can bring us wealth, success, happiness and all the things you've ever dreamed of for you and your family. You chose the right Dragon for you, the Dominating, Delusional, Destructive Dragon or the Delightful, Daring, Dynamic Dragon.

The Dominating Delusional Destructive Dragon in your head can be a huge hindrance in your life, I'm sure you've noticed that?

My goal with this book is to get you to take action, to accomplish the dreams that you have for yourself. When you slay the Dragon in your head you become highly resourceful and successful.

When you are in fear you aren't open to change, it's only the voice inside your head that that creates your fear. While most people are waiting around for the world and it's circumstances to get better, you must be taking the time to get that voice in your head under control, so you can get into action. Only when you get into action will your life change for the better.

Learning to slay the Triple D Dragon in your head is going to put you in that powerful, positive and optimistic and resourceful state.

Each and every one of us has infinite and unlimited potential, everyone one of us has the capability to do far more than what we are currently doing. So what is it that stands in the way of us achieving our full potential?

The answer is simple, *REALITY*. Our own reality stands in the way of us attaining what we want out of life. The reality of our life is the way we individually see the world, this reality stops us from truly living our dream. The only person, who tells you if you're having or experiencing something nice or nasty, is you. Because you are the only person who tells you if something is nice or nasty, you make up your own reality. Everyone experiences things differently in their own way and it's these differences in us all, that create our very own individual feelings which make us take action on our goals or not.

However, there are people on earth who are not stopped by their current reality. Take Roger Bannister for example, the thoughts of all the scientist of that time said the four minute mile could not be broken, they said it just could not be done. They even said that the human body wasn't capable of doing it.

Roger Bannister did it he broke that reality, and once he broke it guess what happened? It broke so many other people's reality. Even children can run a four minute mile now. But back then it wasn't physically possible.

If you look at Arnold Schwarzenegger he was told that he was too late for the movie industry the films of muscle men had been and gone. He was also told he couldn't speak properly because his accent was so strong, he was told he would never be in the movies. These people like Arnold Schwarzenegger and Roger Bannister faced barriers that stopped them each and every single day.

People all around them said *"no, it will never work."* Yet they both did something that so few can do. They created their own new reality. When you create your own reality you instantly turn your potential into a brand new reality for yourself.

The obvious question then is how do you do that?

That's what I teach in my one to one Psychotherapy and Coaching sessions, what I teach my clients is how to take your infinite and unlimited potential and turn it into the reality that you really want, for you and your family.

People who are capable of smashing through their reality, do it in a completely different way. The first thing to do to create your own reality is, you've got to recognise that early on in life you accidentally believed something in life that isn't true about yourself. People who do this realise that their world isn't created but instead create their own reality, they have identified that there is a mistake they made about who they are.

When you can identify the story that you've made up inside your head about yourself, you now have the power to change it.

As you grow up your own individual way of thinking or mindset takes over and I call this the Dominating, Delusional, Destructive Dragon, which is all that talking in your head. If you listen carefully that dragon represents a set of self imposed limitations based on your own misperceptions of you and the way you act or behave towards all different areas of your life.

The Triple D Dragon creates a configuration or set of plans for you to live your life by. The problem is those plans are not the truth, and it becomes your barriers, mental roadblocks or brick walls from living your dreams. So what the most successful people do is they create a new set of plans, which has them living their life of their dreams and goals versus living the life of their fears and doubts of the Triple D Dragon.

If you don't create a technique or a procedure, then you won't be able to break free from the pull of your own misperceptions. The Triple D Dragon will keep you in the world of your fears and doubts spending your whole life doing the same things over and over again and life will quite simply depress you.

The number one mission of the plan or procedure is to move your perspective on life. When you see it for what it is, what it was and what it always will be, you'll suddenly get inspired to see what's on the other side of the brick wall or mental barrier. When you change your perspective with awareness you instantly become flexible.

When you're flexible it reveals a whole new world of options and those options give you the power to make the changes you want. When you change your perspective, automatically you change your emotional response and as we know your emotions control your life as people only make changes in their lives based on how it will make them feel not based on what they know. You will replace fear with power and strength. You will replace doubt with certainty, you replace frustration with excitement. Learning to control your emotions is a master skill and anyone who knows how to create their own reality, knows how to create or control their emotions. It's as simple as that.

Finally when you create a new plan for your life, you move your perspective on your own life. When you learn to control your emotions you automatically take new action. That's what creating your new reality or removing those brick walls and invisible barriers is all about, it's all about taking new action. You'll automatically start doing the things that you wouldn't normally do, because those new actions totally take you to your new Priceless Life Destination.

"You Must Slay That Triple D Dragon Inside Your Head To Become Successful. It's Time To Think Like A Warrior."

Start by seeing yourself as if you have unlimited potential, point this out to that part of your mind that tells you that you are limited. The part I refer to is, that mind that tells you you're not good enough not smart enough, don't have the right education, ugly, stupid or fat. See the Triple D Dragon for what it is and that will get you inspired.

When you see the dragon for what it is, you can become someone who can choose what inspires you. Rather than someone who is possessed by irrational fears or procrastination that stops you dead in your tracks. You can choose actions and new ways of doing things that will inspire you, when you see the dragon for what it is.

Let's take some evaluation of the Triple D Dragon I want you to start by writing down two things that you want to accomplish in the next 2-3 months. What are two things that would make a difference for you and totally change your life for the better?

Is it that you want to make more money? Do want to lose weight? Accomplish a new objective? Is there a new project that you want to start? Do you want to finish something that you've already started? Write them down right now.

The next thing that I want you to write down is, think about what it is that's currently stopping you from accomplishing these things?

Why have you not accomplished these things, these two goals, why? What is it that's getting in your way? Why have you been stopped dead in your tracks, for all this time?

Everything you just wrote down is the Triple D Dragon working his destructive ways in your life. Your very own Triple D Dragon is trying to keep you safe from achieving your dreams.

So what is the Triple D Dragon exactly, it's nothing more than all the reasons why you do what you do. It is the talking in you head, think about it like this The Triple D Dragon is basically all the nag, nag, nag, nag talking in your head and all the images that are going on at the same time as well. Let me explain, you've got images and you've got sounds and they are constantly going non-stop all the time, constantly drawing you towards what the dragon wants for you. I'm sure you've noticed that there is this non stop chatter that is happening in your head, haven't you?

And have you also noticed that this non stop chatter in your head is sort of out of your control? If you think about it like this, our bodies that we live in have created a tool or procedure to protect you. That procedure is all about trying to foresee or envisage and understand what's going to happen next to move you and your body in a specific direction. We've got to start to recognise, it's really just designed to keep you safe. It's there to protect you.

The crazy thing is it's not on your side, have you noticed that? Lets be honest here you lay there at night and you want to go to sleep and guess what the Triple D dragon wont stop talking in your head. It doesn't let you go to sleep, or you'll say "I've got to make this important phone call and what happens, up pops the Dragon talking you out of it.

Have you ever been on a diet before? Who's the first one to talk you out of it? Of course it's the Triple D Dragon. I want you to start to notice that the system of thinking is not there to be on your side, or to help you accomplish your goals. It's there to actually protect you from what it perceives as potential danger.

Now what is potentially dangerous? The things that are potentially dangerous are the things that are unknown to us and the dragon.

Well guess what, have you ever noticed that almost the entire world is unknown to you? Do you know what's going to happen tomorrow or at the weekend or what numbers will come up in the lottery? Of course you don't, this is a huge problem if you want to do big things with your life. If you want to accomplish more and really go for it and live your dreams, you can't let the talking in your head be the thing that is ruling your life. You can't have the dragon as your guide or it will lead you down the wrong path. The only path the dragon will lead you to is mediocrity.

You have to learn to follow your heart or gut feeling and stop listening to the Triple D Dragon. The talking in your head is just your own mindset that you've built up based on experiences you've had in the past. It's part of the system or tools it has to steer you and your body away from potential danger. Now the only problem that you're faced with is your life isn't dangerous. Come on let's get real about it, calling people up on the phone, is that dangerous? Starting something new or taking a step in a project is not dangerous. Asking someone out on a date is not dangerous. Deciding to eat healthy and exercise regularly is not dangerous, it's good for you.

But these are the things the Triple D Dragon talks you out of all day long and these are the things that stop us, from moving our life forward. It stops us from saying yes to the things that will absolutely change our life for the better.

The results you can achieve when you can slay the Triple D Dragon in your head will amaze you, it will cause you to do the things you need to do, to make your goals and dreams just come together. This will create a brand new reality for yourself and your family.

There are two things the Triple D Dragon does to stop you and it's literally a brick wall that you hit every day. I want to show you how to break through it. The way you breakthrough it is with these principles.

First you must become aware and gain awareness, when you know about something you can do something about it, can't you? Awareness makes you flexible and flexibility is the second part of what were going to do. Flexibility leads to new options. So when you become aware you suddenly see the world completely different than you thought before, so it's easier to move around and forward towards your dream life. You then become flexible and it's easier to do the things you couldn't do before.

Doing those new things will then reveal brand new options for you like all of a sudden you start to replace the *"I can't do that"* with *"I can now do this and that"* or even *"I'm now feeling confident that I can do this instead."*

This new power gives you new options and new options give you power. What kind of power? It's simple, the power that you need to change your life and create your own reality.

So let's start by looking at two things you need to be aware of, these new awareness's will be a bit like the foundations of your house. Suddenly the reality that you are living will start to crumble around you. Then you can rebuild it how you want it to look like. Rather than having the Triple D Dragon build it for you accidentally, by bumping around all its life and creating stuff up and keeping you away from it.

The Triple D Dragon is a story teller, what does that mean he's a story teller. It's quite simply a protection mechanism let me explain. I want you to think back when you were a little child and your Mum or Dad told you not to go near an oven or a fire because you'll burn yourself. What was the first thing you did? You went straight over to that fire or oven and burnt your hand. Your heart started pounding and your brain went into overdrive, your subconscious mind turned it's blinkers on and looked for what caused you, the upset feelings and pain. Instantly it connected the fire or oven with the pain and in doing so made a connection between your conscious and subconscious mind.

Instantly The Triple D Dragon says to you *"next time I go near a fire or an oven I'm going to check if the fire or oven is turned on"* So every time you go near a fire or oven you are conditioned from that moment on in your life. You instantly create a thought process inside your head that says *"every time I go near a fire I'm going to check first to see if it's turned on so I won't burn myself again."*

This is really positive I'm sure you'll agree? However when it comes to goal achievement we have a challenge. If you go to stroke a dog and the dog bites you, next time you go to stroke a dog, what do you think? *"All dogs bite, be careful"* But do all dogs bite? Of course they don't. But your mind perceives it to be that way. Very quickly you become a slave to your Dominating, Delusional, Destructive Dragon and your nervous system for connecting it emotionally inside your body.

You begin to live in a figment of your imagination or even a fantasy world, or in other words you're living in a reality that isn't the truth. So how does it act like a story teller? Well it generalises firstly with people, let's say you meet someone for the first time. You immediately come up with a conclusion about who they are and what they do and how they do it. Remember you have not met this person before and you have no idea who people are. But you make up stories in your head about who they are and you don't even catch yourself doing it.

Since you don't catch yourself doing it, you think people are the way they are and that's it and more importantly you believe it to be the truth. But their not, sorry you are not a clairvoyant or a mind reader, you cannot tell who people are just by looking at them. You know this thought that some people have when they say *"I have great understanding of people and I can really read them."* What a load of rubbish!! What you can do is, you can make things up inside your head about what you think they are like. A bit like a child's dot to dot book and then you can con-nect the dots in your mind. But you don't see the truth in people because you don't even know who you are. If you did then you would be able to stop yourself doing the things that you keep putting off wouldn't you?

Now this is the crazy thing, all day long you pretend you know who other people are; *THIS IS KILLING YOUR DREAMS.* Because your dreams come from other people, what do I mean? Well let's think about it for a minute, all of your opportunities come in and from your relationship to others. See that all empowerment is related to other people. So if you are judging people and you don't even notice you are doing it. You need to investigate the things that the Triple D Dragon is saying about other people. Very quickly you'll realise, that you've created all kinds of values, rules, judgements and assessments about all different kinds of people. It just becomes like that and that's the way it is. You don't even notice it going on inside your head and the reason you don't even notice it is because you've done it all your life from a very young child.

Think back to the beginning of the book when I constantly did the same thing. I thought that big businesses didn't do business with small businesses. I had created judgements, assessments and values on big businesses that simply weren't true. It was only when I caught myself doing it, that I could question it and change my future.

It becomes the trap that you're living in, you don't even notice you're walking around not noticing what you're doing and then all of a sudden you become aware of it. In my therapy and coaching sessions I remove the shield of significance which is what I call it. That's what we all see the world through, and when clients see it they say *"I can't believe I did that, where did that come from?"* When you just let it go and realise what you've been doing all your life, you can move forward.

The moment you see all the judgements and the assessments and evaluations you've made about people is the moment that you can choose to become flexible.

The second area that use story telling ineffectively is in situations, let me explain you won't go into a situation because you foresee or make up a fantasy world saying to yourself *"well I remember that similar situation before and this is what happened then. So it's obvious it will turn out the same way again for me."* This is what everyone does and it stops you from living your Priceless Life.

Now rather than finding out, guess what you do? You speculate, rather than finding out you hallucinate. Speculation is not good for living your dreams; do you know what it's good for? Staying alive and the problem is you're not in a dangerous situation. Your life is not filled with danger. You are getting stopped and stuck constantly by the dragon in your head.

The Next Thing The Triple D Dragon Does is:

The Triple D Dragon is a negative future dragon. This quite simply means The Triple D dragons job is to investigate or think through the worst thing that could possibly happen to you. When you do something how often do you think to yourself what's the worst thing that could happen and then you don't even do it. I'm guessing for some of you this is a regular occurrence. However as I'm sure you'll agree this is a terrible trait for attracting your Priceless Life

Let's think about it in this way, what is the point of the negative future Dragon? It's simple we look at things, we smell them we investigate things and in our minds we prophesise or make stuff up, about whether it will be good for us or not. It's the same thing when we're out in the world we're investigating and utilising our senses to prophesise and get a feel for which is the best thing for us to do. Our bodies are not really well equipped to put up with a lot of pain. We get hurt very easily; we get cut or grazed easily, we break bones very easily. So what we have developed is an ability to investigate the world in our mind and through our mind by thinking up what's the worst that could happen.

What it means is we don't spend much time actually living in reality; you spend all of your time in your head in your own reality. Deciphering the information back and forth, back and forth, thinking about whether or not if it's a good idea for us to do something or not.

Let's say you have this new goal to bring a new product out or start a new business. What does the Triple D Dragon do? It says to you inside your head *"no one is going to like it anyway; you don't know what you're doing. People aren't going to take me seriously and nobody is going to buy it anyway"* it just goes on and on and then you say *"you know what, I think I'll just go and watch television."*

Has it ever occurred to you that putting things off until tomorrow is actually a survival tool that you've inherently built in yourself. That procrastination occurs when the negative future dragon kicks in and starts all of his destructive ways. I see so many people that just don't ask for what they want. Why? Because they already know in advance they are just not going to get it. Well I'm here to tell you that is just a lie that you tell yourself and it's that lie that has always stopped you.

This must of happened to you loads of times you get an invitation or something like that and it says you should do this or have you tried that and the Triple D Dragon in your head says *"no thanks, I can't do it"* Remember you don't know if you can actually do it or not. You're not a clairvoyant, you can't tell the future, but you pretend that you can. If you've never been there before nor done it before, how on earth do you know. The crazy thing is just because you tried it once and failed doesn't mean the next time you try it, you won't succeed does it?

Have you noticed that you actually pretend that you are clair-voyant or can read people minds or see into the future? The truth is, you are making things up all day long and you don't even know that you are doing it. The crazy thing is that the things you make up don't serve you or empower you or even help you.

There are so many things that you don't know, it's unbelievable and one of the biggest things you don't know is that you were and have been conditioned like a pet. You were literally domes-ticated wee over here, pooh over there, walk like this, talk like that, and believe these things, hang around with these type of people. You don't believe the things you believe, because you want to believe them; you believe those things because you were domesticated through pain and pleasure from an early age and you continued to learn this way.

What we all need to understand is this, people in life are just out in the world doing whatever they are doing, living their life in their own way and you're making up endless stories about them and the things that they do. Remember you are not the ruler of the universe and everyone in it, are you? But I bet you behave that way don't you? Let me explain what I mean.

You don't decide how people are supposed to behave do you. You also don't decide how people are supposed to operate or do things in their lives; you don't decide what they are supposed to do. You don't decide how they are supposed to talk, walk, dress, move or any of those things, do you? But you get so mad and upset and angry every single time somebody breaks your expectations don't you?

Where did your expectations of life and other people and circumstances come from? You made them up inside your head; your Triple D Dragon took over this process for you. Remember they don't exist they are not real. But they mess with your emotions and get you into fear, anger, self doubt, upset and worry. Remember you don't know the rules of what other peoples life should be like or behave like or even how life should be.

Your Triple Dragon even works when you go out, have you noticed that when you go to events or to a restaurant, you instantly start to talk to yourself inside your head *"that's not right, that's in the wrong place and I don't know why they are doing that or he's looking at me that way. Who in their right mind would think those colours would match with that."* It's a bit like you walk in and the Triple D Dragon goes no, no, no, no, no, no. It's constantly on the negative output mode trying to find everything that you don't like. Then you wonder why opportunities don't come your way. You wonder why you're not an invitation or a welcoming place for living your dream life.

It's all because you're letting the Triple D Dragon run the show and he's judging, assessing, evaluating, making things up and just being a mean nasty horrible idiot, breathing his fire over all different areas of your life.

There is not a correct way to live life. Look you may think your way is right but I'm here to tell you there is not a correct way to live life. There's your way, there's the way that you have invented but that's not the right way. There's the way that your parents taught you but that's not the right way. There's the way that you've kind of bumped into things and made decisions and choices along the way, but that's not the right way. Have you ever investigated it or even thought about it? I don't think that you have and because you haven't and definitely haven't thought it through properly or how it might work for other people, you can't be imposing your stuff on other people because when you do it pushes them away.

If you push people away, then you push opportunities away as well. If you push opportunities away you're not going to live the life that you want. What it really comes down to is being the type of person who invites, who brings good stuff into their lives. When you practise having total acceptance of all people just watch what happens I promise you your life will change, magic will just happen.

So How Do We Control The Dominating, Delusional Destructive Dragon?

Step 1 – Realise That Your Mind (The Dominating Delusional Destructive Dragon) is Not Your Friend, He's definitely Not On Your Side.

Your mind, which I call The Dominating, Delusional Destructive Dragon, (The Triple D Dragon) doesn't care about your goals and dreams. Have you ever noticed that when you set new goals and new dreams, the first person to talk you out of it is the self talk in your head?

Firstly remember the Dominating, Delusional, Destructive Dragon isn't your friend, how do I know that? Well who else do you allow in your life to call you fat, a failure, worthless, a waste of space no good for nothing, I'm not good enough, I'm not smart enough? Nobody right...

You allow your mind the Triple D Dragon to talk to you like this though, don't you? If anyone in real life talked to you like this, you'd either fight with them or never be their friend ever again. You allow the Triple D Dragon to do this everyday to you, don't you?

When you go on a diet, what does the Dominating, Delusional, Destructive Dragon do? It tells you to eat cake, crisps and biscuits. What type of a friend would do that?

It never ever stops talking to you about other people's behaviour, it says things like *"I can't believe he did that or she talked to me like that and did that to me"* or *"I can't believe he looked at me like that."*

Have you ever stayed awake all night long talking to yourself just because the Triple D Dragon won't shut up? Have you tried to shut it up but it keeps talking to you about all different kinds of rubbish and other people who've you met that day and stuff you've watched on television? Of course you have, I'm sure everyone has sometime in their lives been fed up with their own Triple D Dragon.

Have you ever gone into a restaurant or a room full of total strangers and instantly without meeting that person just by looking at them you've said to yourself hmmm I'm not going to like them.

We all do this, and this is the Triple D Dragon at play working his evil ways to destroy your life.

Have you ever read a text or a letter or an email from someone and they used two words that made you feel angry or upset at what they were saying? That's your Triple D Dragon working his magic, destroying your life.

Have you ever thought to yourself that someone doesn't like you and you are certain beyond a shadow of a doubt that it's true? That's your Triple D Dragon again.

Have you ever gone somewhere maybe a gym a function, networking meeting or a restaurant and felt self aware that everyone is looking at you. Have you ever felt you're not good enough and you feel embarrassed. That's your Triple D Dragon working his evil ways again and again.

Have you ever felt that your parents love your brother or sister more than they do you? Have you ever felt that your brother or sister or your friends are so much better at everything than you are? The triple D Dragon is always there telling you the things you don't want to hear all day long.

The Triple D Dragon wants to keep you safe and steer you away from the unknown, it's not interested in you achieving your goals or your dreams. Its main function is to keep you away from the worst thing that can happen, so you don't end up looking like a fool. Or embarrass yourself in front of people you don't even know or care about. Which makes you give up before you try.

I don't care how confident you think you are, you are always battling your dragon inside your head.

You are a bit like The Triple D Dragons puppet, it steers you away from danger and pulls the strings in your life called fear, anger, self doubt, frustration and apprehension.

You are a prisoner of your mind and a slave to the Triple D Dragon.

Step 2 – Realise There Are Two Dragons In Your Life, (Just like The Yin & Yang)

It is so important that you begin to see that there are two dragons. There is The Dominating, Delusional, and Destructive Dragon. This is a non-stop talking dragon that never shuts up, has an opinion on everything and everyone and even has opinions on things it knows nothing about. Then there is the dragon who is listening, which is who you really are. Your goal is to begin to realise that there is constant talking in your head, which is really trying to keep you safe. Then there is a dragon who is listening which is trying to have an amazing life.

These two elements are opposing against each other. The dragon who is listening has surrendered control of your life on accident; it's just let it all happen. In order for you to achieve happiness and success, you have got to stop trusting in the mind and start listening to that part of you that knows what's best for you. Your gut feeling will say *"yes I can do this."* Then your mind will think of a million reasons why you can't. Your gut feeling will say, *"Take the action, say yes, go for it. Let's start that diet or let's start that business, that I've always been putting off"* and your mind will say, *"You are not good enough, you're stupid, you have done it in the past and it didn't work out then, so it won't this time."*

Start by really noticing that the mind's job is to keep you safe; it's a part of your own thought processes and patterns that you've installed. Notice that today, and watch how it brings relief and it will bring more happiness.

Start to recognise that all your suffering that you constantly deal with, is just your own meaning of your opinion. All opinions are nothing more than a guesstimation of the mind about the truth of reality. Reality cannot be distinguished or separated from the mind. The mind sees life through a filter called your very own perception.

I know it sounds like psychotherapy mumbo jumbo, but if you read those words over and over again. I promise a transformation will start to occur within you. A brand new you will begin to appear, a happier, more fulfilled, more satisfied version of yourself will start to appear. Someone who is encouraged and empowered, willing to take risks and willing to take action on things that you previously were afraid to take action on will emerge. So I really encourage you to take five minutes and read those words again, because when you truly get it and what it really means. It will just fall into place for you and you'll gain an understanding of why you are where you are in life, under the teachings of your Triple D Dragon.

For you to become successful and happy, I want you to begin to notice that The Triple D Dragon _(all that talking in your head)_ is not on your side and doesn't care about your goals and dreams. This will give you the energy and the enthusiasm to stop listening to the mind and start listening to your gut feeling or instinct. Or what I like to call it the Delightful, Daring, Dynamic Dragon. This is the dragon you must take more notice of.

Step 3 – The Triple D Dragon Is A Storyteller (it quite simply makes stuff up)

If you've ever taken any of my courses before or seen me on a 1-2-1 basis, then you'll know your mind which I call the Dominating, Delusional, Destructive Dragon (The Triple D Dragon.) Is not a great loving friend for achieving your dreams or your Priceless Life

Its sole purpose is to keep you alive and one of its tools it uses is to make up negative events about the future. It makes up negative things that will happen so you don't even try or give it a go. It does this so you'll avoid them and never even try them. What do I mean by this? Well just think back to the beginning of the book.

I made up a story that I couldn't knock on big companies' doors, all because the dragon had told me that big businesses don't do business with small businesses. It had totally fabricated the future. It told me not to even try because if you do, you'll be just like a fool. The dragon is constantly building up reference and evidence all throughout your life and storing it away inside your subconscious mind. It remembers everything that someone's told you and I mean everything especially the negative things. Let's say for instance if another person tried something and was unsuccessful. It is always looking out and searching for the worst possible thing that could happen, so it can say to you *"told you so, if they can't do it. Neither can you."*

Let me tell you something right now, there is no worst case scenario coming your way. Why? Because your life, just like everyone else's is on a journey of growth, development, more knowledge, more experiences. What do I mean by that well do you still believe in Santa Claus?

Of course you don't, but at one time in your life you did didn't you? All because powerful people in your life told you he was true, your parents, grand parents, teachers, school friends and even the television, tell us Santa Claus exists and he's real. We build up lots of reference and evidence even before Christmas arrives that Santa Claus is true don't we? Then on Christmas morning we wake up and magically all our presents have been delivered, and some presents even say lots of love from Santa Claus. Instantly we believe it to be true, the Triple D Dragon buys into the whole magic of Santa Claus and he does this because, not only have we got powerful people in our lives telling us Santa

Claus is real but we've then had evidence that he exists when we've woken up on Christmas morning.

When we return to school after the Christmas holidays all our school friends have had the same experience, we share our stories of Christmas and what Santa Claus brought us for Christmas. This gains more power for the subconscious mind as it's more and more evidence and reference. We lock it inside our subconscious minds and we totally believe that Santa Claus is true. All because we've built up all the evidence that we need to and we buy into the whole concept, don't we?

Then What Happens?

We then get older a few years down the line and a child in the playground tells us Santa Claus is a load of rubbish and it's just Mum and Dad. At first we don't believe it, but we ask our parents and when they tell us the truth, instantly we see it for what it is and we let go of it and never believe it ever again. So we are constantly learning, constantly developing and constantly growing all the time. As a grown adult you wouldn't believe in all the things that you once believed as a child or a teenager would you?

Your Dominating, Delusional and Destructive Dragon is always telling you that if you did this, or if you did that then you could lose everything. If you lost everything, your house, your job, you car, your lifestyle, could you get it all back? Of course you could, we often hear of multi millionaires who've lost everything two or even three times in their career and gained it all back again haven't we.

The Triple D Dragon is a complete idiot, it keeps saying to you *"I don't think we'll get it all back, I don't want to lose it all"*

How many times have you heard someone say they want to set up their own business but there's always been this block holding them back saying *"I'll lose my house I won't be able to pay* my mortgage." If that was true would anybody have their own business of course they wouldn't we would all be working for the government wouldn't we?

So the Triple D Dragon is a story teller, it literally just makes things up. So don't avoid the worst case scenario. Go straight forward towards it.

Step 4 – Accept It For What It Is a destructive part of you)

Accept the situation as it is.....

Let's start by getting the dominating delusional dragon under control

Put procedures into place that consistently confronts and slays the dragon

Take action however small it is, do it now to slay that dragon. Put your life on a different pathway and you'll transform that fear into action by taking consistent baby steps every day.

There is no failure just feedback.

This is so important to control the Triple D dragon we have to stop telling ourselves that we've failed at something, because the Triple D Dragon just loves the word failure. It is his favourite word of all time; he's looking out for it all day long, so he can build up even more evidence and reference of why you shouldn't try to attempt to go out of your comfort zone. Because he wants you to stay where it's safe away from the unknown, somewhere where it's easy and life just plods on by.

So we must change the way we communicate with ourselves. If we fail at something or hear about someone who's failed at something, just say to yourself *"that wasn't a failure I just learnt a new way of how not to do it. And smart people learn from their mistakes"*

The Dominating, Delusional, Destructive Dragon doesn't care if you are happy, satisfied, loving life, fulfilled, in love or living your dream. The Dominating, Delusional, Destructive dragons job is to assess the situation and move you out of the way away from danger and harm and towards pleasure to keep you alive, that's what the dominating dragons job is. If you don't make a conscious effort to stop its destruction, it will blow its fire all over your life and you'll get burnt.

The Dominating, Delusional, Destructive Dragon is part of you, it's always been there. It's a bit like your dna and you've accidentally thought of it as you. The is because since you were a young child it's constantly talked to you all day long and you've let it control you. Scientific tests show that every eleven seconds we talk to ourselves and 80% of that inner talk we have with ourselves is negative. So 80% of the time the Dominating, Delusional, Destructive Dragon is doing its thing, working it's destruction in your life.

Step 5 The Triple D Dragon Has An Opinion On Everything And Anything. (Get over it, just let it go)

Get over it, the Dominating, Delusional, and Destructive Dragons opinion won't change. Its opinions are the source of your suffering. It's only the dragons opinion that is causing your life to suffer. It's only your defiance to what has been sown by the dragon, what is causing you to suffer.

This is my favourite part about the Triple D Dragon; it has an opinion on *EVERYTHING* and *ANYTHING* including all the things it knows nothing about. This is a total joke, but until it's brought to your attention you don't even catch yourself doing it.

Have you ever noticed that there have been loads of times in your life when you know absolutely nothing about a certain subject? You've never even had a conversation about it before. You've not gained even the slightest bit of evidence about it, but you say *"I know and I know that I know and I also know that you definitely do not know."* I see this happening every single day, how many times will someone say *"I'm not trying that it's just not right for me"* it could be food or a certain sporting activity. It could even be a certain shop that we don't like to shop in.

Now the crazy thing is we've already made up our minds before we've even tried it, especially with food people will say *"I don't like beetroot"* even if they haven't tried or ever tasted it before. Remember the Triple D Dragon has an opinion on anything and everything and thinks it knows best all of the time.

We Are Constantly On The Defensive From Things & People That Aren't Attacking Us.

We're dealing with our own issues of self-realisation; each and every one of us sees the world in our own individual unique way. We are all living inside our heads rather than living in the real reality of life. The opinions that we have allowed the dragon to make up, are our own world. We are all trying to protect ourselves from all types of different things. Someone could look at you in a certain way and you say to yourself *"I know what that look means."* There is no way we know what that look means, just by the way someone looks at us. We perceive things in our own ways, due to the way we've collected evidence and reference in our lives.

Our Triple D Dragon has logged and remembered everything and stored it away. It does this in a millisecond so it can make up its mind on things that happened to us or things that happened to other people in the past. That evidence it recalls tells us how to cope with a certain situation and which action we'll take. We take on other peoples opinions all the time, I see other peoples opinions as breaking wind they come out when you don't want them to and they stink up your mind.

You continue to send yourself false messages all day long because the Triple D Dragon acts upon all the things he's stored away for all these years.

Even young children at an early age as 3 or 4 have their own dragons working against them. They start to become self aware and won't sing or perform in front of family, friends or other children because they feel that they will laugh at them. So stop protecting yourself from people who aren't trying to hurt you.

Step 6 Making The Same Mistake Twice
(if you do what you've always done,
you'll always get the same results)

The Triple D Dragon is constantly in the avoidance mode of trying to stop making the same mistake twice. It's constantly looking at this present moment in time and it's seeing how it relates to the past and then it will come up with a generalisation or a guesstimate of what it should do now.

The Triple D Dragon lives in a reality where it says to you *"if this happened last time it will obviously happen again."*

Let me ask you these questions

Are you a clairvoyant?

Can you see into the future?

Can you read peoples minds?

Do you know beyond a shadow of a doubt what will happen tomorrow?

Of course not you aren't any of the above; we all make the future up for ourselves inside our own heads. We simply make things up about the future and a lot of the time we do it so we won't feel bad, for not being the person that we've always wanted to be. Far too often we find ourselves making up all different kinds of excuses of why we just can't do what needs to be done. These are excuses or just stories or things that the Triple D Dragon has made up. So there is no future, it's just the things we've made up and whatever we focus on we become. Whatever we focus on, we actually attract more of it into our lives.

So if we continue to keep telling ourselves *"I can't do this because of that"* or *"this will never happen to me,"* or *I'm just not that type of person, luck doesn't happen to me."* That's why you are, where you are in life today.

Henry Ford Said. "Whether you think you can or you can't you're right."

So if there is no future only what we make up. Now you realise that, why not make up a future that will be awesome. Now this can only happen when you catch the Triple D Dragon in the act trying to avoid making the same mistake twice. You have to catch it in the act that's the only way.

In alcoholics anonymous they say you can't control the first thought but you can control the second. Thoughts are automatic, they're just happening all the time. So always be aware of what you say to yourself, this isn't easy and I'll tell you why. It's because you've done it for so long and it's been natural for you for so long. Now is the time to become aware of what it says and when it says it, then change the words and the thought process.

Have you ever noticed the Triple D Dragon doesn't listen to you? This is how it works, lets say you go out somewhere and it says to you *"look at that person over there what's wrong with the clothes they are wearing and their hair is such a mess, they must of got dressed in the dark."* You then say to yourself *"stop judging people,"* but it doesn't listen does it? It literally operates 100% all the time automatically.

You're not even in charge of your own body, here's a quick experiment just close your eyes and I want you to just notice how your body is continuously doing stuff without you. Your facial expressions, your breathing, your smiles, giggles, blinking of your eyes. The small little itches and twitches you have.

Are you doing any of that? *NO!!!!*

When you walk do you make a conscious effort to think about placing one foot in front of the other? No of course you don't, it just happens automatically for you doesn't it? I want you to begin to recognise that this Dominating, Delusional Destructive Dragon has been controlling you from birth.

Take a minute now and try and stop breathing can you do it? No, you have to start breathing; you can only hold your breath for so long. Then the body kicks in and says "Hello, *you are going to start breathing now."*

Remember the Triple D Dragon is in a perpetual state of predicting negative futures for you. When it does this the negative futures that you are trying to avoid by actually focusing on them you pull them straight to you, just like a magnet.

How many times have you heard about cancer sufferers who have never been told about their illness for years? Then as soon as they are told only a matter of weeks later they die. All because what ever we focus our thoughts on, we attract into our lives.

Dogs when they have cancer live for years all because no one has ever told them....

The Triple D Dragon will often say to you *"it's a good thing I'm around. I'll always look after you and steer you in the right direction."* I really want you to remember this because it's so important. Everything that bothers worries or concerns you in your life you created yourself and by trying to avoid it, you've had to concentrate on it. So by actually trying to avoid it you've attracted it straight towards you. Can you see how important this is and why you are where you are in life today?

What happens in car crashes, how many times do you see cars that have hit lamp posts or other cars? It's because we say to ourselves whilst the crash is taking place *"don't hit that lamp post"* or *"don't hit that car"* over and over again and what happens, we hit it. Whatever we think about or say in our heads, we'll attract into our lives.

Let me tell you a story that's only just happened to me recently in the last few weeks. I was out shopping with my family the other week and we came across a jewellery shop and saw this Swarovski bracelet. There was no price on the bracelet so we went inside and asked the price of the bracelet. It was very expensive for what it was, but was very beautiful. We didn't buy the bracelet, but since then we've seen that bracelet everywhere. Film stars wear them celebrities on television we've seen wearing them and even television presenters. All of a sudden it's as if this bracelet is everywhere.

Now the question is this; were those bracelets there before? Of course they were but our mind didn't see them before. Once it's seen something and remembers it it's on the look out trying to find it everywhere. Before your dragon knew they existed, that part of your mind wasn't open to it and because it wasn't open to it, you never saw it before.

The Triple D Dragon is all about keeping you the same, making sure you stay safe by not doing anything new. He loves to identify patterns or familiarity, identifying them and then making sure you repeat them over and over again.

Do you ever notice that there are some common themes or patterns in your life; do you keep dating the same type of people? Do you keep marrying the same type of person? Do you keep having the same type of friends and experiences? You can have new situations but the experience will be the same, that's because the Triple D Dragon loves similarity. He loves things to be the same again and again so you won't venture out of your comfort zone, because your dragon thinks that by doing so, you'll stay safe.

Who you are is a function of the domestication that your parents and your family unit put you through. So who and what you are is nothing more than an erasing machine, you delete everyone and everything. What do I mean by this? Let me explain. All of us delete certain places and people out of our lives so we'll feel confident that it's ok for us. Based on this, our individual dragons decide on how and whom you talk to; who you should interact with, who you should have as a friend, who you should tell your secrets to. We make our mind up about someone in an instant even before we've talked to them. Just by looking at them we've totally made up our mind in a matter of seconds if we'll like them or not. All because of the programming we've had and this is what I want to cover next.

A Quick Summary Of How To Slay
The Dominating Delusional Destructive Dragon.

- First Realise that your mind is not your friend.
- Remember its job is to keep you safe away from the unknown, so you won't try anything new or jump out of your comfort zone.

- There are two dragons and you can choose which one to listen to.
- The Triple D Dragon makes things up that aren't true, he's a story teller
- The Triple D Dragon will always self prophesise that there's a worse case scenario
- It will try to protect us against people who aren't attacking us.
- It has an opinion about anything and everything and even the stuff it knows nothing about.
- It thinks it knows best all the time.
- It's always on the lookout for the negative in everything.
- It always wants to make the same mistake twice.
- YOU MUST CATCH THE DOMINATING, DELUSIONAL DESTRUCTIVE DRAGON DOING ITS STUFF.

CHAPTER SEVEN

My T.F.A.B. Formula To Success.

Nothing is either good or bad, but thought makes it so.

William Shakespeare

There's a formula that I use which I call the TFAB formula. We've learnt what the Dominating, Delusional, Destructive Dragon does and how and why he does it. This section is all about the programming it's had.

When I first started to work on myself and transform my life and become successful. This is without a shadow of a doubt, the number one key ingredient that leads to becoming successful in any area of your life. When I started using this very powerful technology on my own belief systems and behaviours, this was when I found out about, who I was and where I was going. That's when my life changed for the better.

I then started showing other people what I was doing and how my life was changing. Very quickly they started to implement the TFAB technologies and they quickly started getting on track and started turning their life around as well.

I've helped thousands of clients by using the same principles and methodologies of changing the way you think, towards becoming successful or wealthy. Whatever it is you want to change for the better in your life the way you think about it, ends up determining your success.

The formula I use which I call the TFAB Formula is like everything else that works, is simple to use. Your Thoughts lead to your Feelings which lead to your Actions which lead to your Behavioural patterns.

That's the process of manifestation and many other people use a version of that or something similar. Except there's one little twist that I use that makes all the difference in the world, where does the whole process start from? Well looking at this chart it all appears that the whole process starts from your thoughts.

Well you couldn't be farther away from the truth; it's not your thoughts. Because what is it that leads to your thoughts? What is it that leads to the way that you think?

The answer to that is the key to everything, the secret that you've bought this book for. The answer is your programming and your conditioning, it's what you learnt when you were young and what you're learning throughout your entire life each and everyday.

We've all been programmed from an early age to the present day on the way we look at things, the way we feel about certain places, the way we act towards certain people or situations.

This programming or what I like to call viruses we've installed into our own subconscious minds has come from our own individual experiences when we tried something and succeeded or failed. Our individual programming/viruses of when we attended a certain function or meeting and felt nervous have had a huge knock on effect on our lives. Our own individual programming/viruses that we make up inside our heads, for what has to happen for us so we'll know it feels just right.

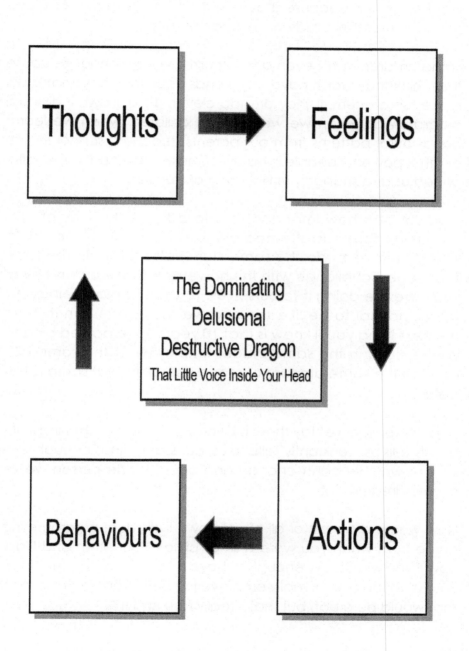

It's our own individual programming/viruses about how you feel when you go to the dentist or standing in front of a group of people and talking or singing. We all know many children that don't want to do this because they feel they'll make a fool of themselves or the other children will laugh at them.

Some children don't even apply themselves at school, because they think they won't have any friends as all their classmates will make fun of them, if they are too clever. It's our own individual programming when we were young children, when we learnt behavioural patterns from our parents, teachers, school friends or other powerful people in our lives. These powerful people influenced us and shaped our own way of thinking.

Can you see how important it is to address this way of programming that has affected our lives right now. If we don't, we'll continue to do the same stuff we've done in the past. The biggest challenge with this however is that we don't even know we are doing it to ourselves. To us as human beings, it's totally normal to be like this and we never question it. Then the next thing you'll know is that 10 years have passed by and you're stuck in the same place, employed at the same job, earning the same amount of money, stuck in that same rut as before.

And the reason we stay there is because that programming constantly tells us, constantly talks to us, constantly finds enough reasons of why we can't change and become the person we've always dreamed of.

Now where did most or all of your own individual programming come from when you were a small child? Your Mum and Dad, now if you were lucky enough to have a Mum and Dad that filled you full to the brim of really empowering beliefs or programs then that would be great, but that's really rare isn't it?

I think the vast amount of your programming they installed into you came into two categories there were programs to keep you safe or programs to stop you being disappointed.

It's a bit like the young child being really excited and bouncy and going up to his Dad and saying *"Dad I want to be an astronaught"* and his Dad says *"don't be stupid son, you come from Manchester"* as human beings we buy into that don't we. Because someone powerful in our life tells us we can't do it, we believe it to be true and we lock it away in our subconscious minds forever. This couldn't be any further from the truth. The fact is that someone's Son or Daughter <u>will</u> become an astronaught.

So lets take a minute and think of those programs that have been installed by your parents and how they've affected you and the way that you act. Remember it's that programming that has got you to where you are in your life today. If your programming was different then you would be in a completely different place right now in your life.

When you think about those programs it's hard to know which ones were installed by whom, as often we install different programs into our subconscious mind all the time.

The first part of the process which in the critical and crucial change process is to

Create Awareness

What is it I mean by creating awareness?

If you don't realise what's happened to you and become aware that you have been programmed to think in a certain way and therefore act in a certain way in response to that. Then you're going to be blind to it for the rest of your life.

You have to catch yourself doing it, now this is the part where you've got to listen to what you say to yourself and why you say it all the time. Constantly questioning what you believe to be true.

All day long we talk to ourselves that dominating delusional destructive dragon which is what I call your internal voice or your mind is constantly in the "on" switch all day and night long.

The second part is understanding, what it is that you've been programmed with and who did the programming and why they did the programming. What you have to remember is they didn't do that to hurt you for the most part, they did it because that's all they knew at the time and passed their own individual learning's onto you.

There are three key elements to conditioning.

- Number one is verbal conditioning, what you heard as you were growing up from your parents or other powerful people in your life.
- Number two is modelling, what did you see when you were young what behavioural patterns did your parents or other powerful people have towards money or success.
- Number three is experience, what did you experience or specific incidents around all different areas of your life such as money, success, wealth etc.

Those three key elements are what drives peoples thoughts and therefore peoples actions around all different areas of their lives and they don't even know it's happening to them.

WHY? Because it's all locked in inside your subconscious mind at such an early age and the older you get you continue to obtain more and more reference and evidence of the way that you look at the world. You then continue to lock in more and more "*stuff*" to reinforce your outside world and how you see it.

The first element
Verbal conditioning

Verbal conditioning is what you heard from your parents, your friends, your Grandparents, your teachers, your family unit, aunties, uncles and other powerful people in your life at an early age.

Whatever language patterns they used with you in your early years formed a lot, if not all of your opinions on whether or not you can achieve a specific outcome in your life. It even formed your opinion on who to vote for in the general elections

As I said earlier when you were growing up the things your parents said to you can be categorised into two camps.

- Things to stop you being disappointed.
- Things to keep you safe.

When your parents told you things to stop you being disappointed, it really set in a program that you instantly installed into your subconscious mind to not to try. For instance at school sports days what do most parents say to their child? *"just try your best & if you don't win don't worry. At least you gave it your best shot."* Now the reason this is said, is so if the child loses the race then they won't get upset about it. However the opposite happens, this actually installs into the brain the following command *"oh well, if I don't win it doesn't matter"* so the child doesn't really give it their best effort after all.

This command gets locked into the subconscious mind over and over again every sports day. Each time you don't win your Mother gives you a big hug and tells you *"don't worry."* I'm sure you already know that each time you received a loving cuddle from your Mother, you enjoyed it and it gave you a certain connection with her. So you were actually being rewarded for failing!!!

The Second Element
Modelling

Modelling is what you saw when you were young, what behavioural patterns did your parents or other powerful people have towards money or success.

Whatever you saw from your own family unit or teachers or other powerful people in your life when you were growing up, has a massive impact on the way you see the world through your own eyes. If your powerful people in your life never strived for success or material things, or thought and said that *"people who are wealthy are only born into it or are born with a silver spoon in their mouths."* Then quite simply a part of you will believe that to be true.

There will be a part in your subconscious mind where you've locked it away to tell you that this is true and no matter what happens in your life, until you wake up to the fact that this is happening you won't get over it. It will always be a mental roadblock, brick wall or an invisible barrier. This will happen because you will be living inside your head and not in real life.

If the powerful people in your life thought and said to you on a regular basis *"the world doesn't give opportunities for people like us."* Or *"We've never had the lucky breaks in our family"* or *"No one from our family has ever been successful"* or *"We just aren't from a clever family."* Or similar quotes or self prophesising then this will and has had a massive effect on the way you live your life, because you will have locked away in your subconscious mind these phrases and the Triple D Dragon is always looking out for the negative. Your dragon will say to you *"told you so ha, ha, you should have listened to me. Fancy thinking you could amount to something in your life."*

All of these phrases that you would have heard would have made the powerful people in your life behave in a certain way and never push their own comfort zones. They would have continuously argued for their limitations and would have repeatedly done the same thing over and over again trying to get a different result, which we all know doesn't work.

The Third Element
Your Own Experience

Your Own Experience is what we personally got from our own experiences emotionally, how it made us feel and what we believed it to be like. What we saw someone close to us experience and we believed to be true.

Each and every one of us sees the world through our own eyes, and because we see the world through our own eyes we place a certain amount of significance on certain areas of our lives. The same event can happen to two different people but they can both give it different meanings. Those meanings that they give it will make them act and behave in a certain way. All because of the meaning they gave it. This is important, it's that meaning in your life that whatever your family or powerful people in your life had experienced in the past, that will and would have had a similar meaning for you. This happens because when you watched them you will pick up their behavioural patterns.

How many times have you caught yourself saying *"I've done that just like my Dad/Mum would have done it."* I'm sure you've said that to yourself loads of times.

Now before you all call your parents up on the phone and tell them it's their fault why you've not achieved your goals. They only went on what they were told or by what they experienced or saw or heard from their family unit or powerful people in their life and simply didn't know any better.

We are all the sum of our own thinking and programming we had when we were younger and continued to add to, until this present moment.

All the programming we've had comes from all sorts of areas in our lives from the television, newspapers, friends, family and even people who we have a chat with on a one off basis. We take on their opinions and as you now know those opinions were programmed by someone else.

It's a bit like you couldn't do that because I had a friend who did that once and he didn't make it happen for him. So you've got no chance, as human beings we buy into that way of thinking don't we?

Uncertainty Taking Action

Are you uncertain about something in your life right now?

All of us are uncertain about something in our lives, if we weren't then we'd already have it wouldn't we?

My advice or my suggestion is really quite simple *JUST DO IT*. Do whatever you are uncertain about, but do it consistently and persistently.

Why?

Because just by taking the action in just doing it, you actually get in the race and the problem with most people is they just don't start or get off the starting blocks. They don't get in the race they sit back worrying, stressing out or make up lots and lots of excuses of why they shouldn't do it. They get stuck in the starting blocks, wishing their lives were different.

In other words they aren't in the game they are just in their own head and as we all know, real life doesn't happen in your head. It happens in reality in real life by getting in the game. Most of our planning, worrying about and considering about or contemplating about what's going to happen or what could happen. They just don't get into the happening or the actualisation of it.

So you've got to get in the game or get in the now, and correct along the way rather than staying in your head arguing for your limitations before you get into it. Which is what most people do and that's why they never start and if you aim at nothing you'll always hit your target every time.

You must focus your mind on the present moment because that's all that matters.

Let's say you're overweight and you want to lose some weight and you don't like the fact that you're fat. Now you know you should do something to lose weight just sitting on the sofa watching television eating un-healthy snacks isn't going to make it happen. Rather than listening to that voice inside your head that keeps coming up with reasons of why you just can't be bothered, if you don't like the fact that your voice or your mind is loud and obnoxious and negative all the time. Then you should do something to train it to be quiet and supportive to help you attain the weight you want.

There is no worry or anxiety in the moment, when you make a conscious decision to just do it, the worry or anxiety goes away. Success is doing what failures won't do. Listen to that voice or that Triple D Dragon and no matter what it says or tells you, just do it.

CHAPTER EIGHT

I Can't Do That !

It is not the strongest of the species that survives, nor the most intelligent that survives.
It is the one that is the most adaptable to change

Charles Darwin

Far too often I hear people say again and again *"I can't do it"* or *"I can't do that"* or *"I'm not very good at that"* or *"I'm just not talented when it comes to that"* or *"Don't ask me to do that for you, because I'm no good at it"*

This is quite simply a rationalisation or a justification about yourself and your abilities. This is a trap so many people fall into. I'm here to tell you, that you are so much better than you think you are. Possibly your worst decision you could ever make is to tell yourself you're not good at something, because it will hold you back for the rest of your life.

The only thing that's stopped you being good at a particular thing is the skill you needed to learn, THAT'S IT just the skill you needed to learn. How many times do you hear people say *"I'm not very good when it comes to computers, I don't understand them very well."* The only thing or secret ingredient that is lacking is taking a quick course on computers. Anyone can learn about anything these days, with the internet and you tube it's everywhere. Remember the only thing stopping you, is you and your ability to learn a simple skill that's readily available. Just by applying yourself and staying dedicated and determined you'll become competent.

You must have heard the old saying practise makes perfect, well amateurs practise until they get it right while professionals practise until they can't get it wrong.

Whenever you do start to practise or learn a new skill it's obvious you are going to do it pretty badly. You will feel strange, awkward and clumsy and you'll feel angry with yourself for not being able to do it. You'll feel inferior or sometimes silly and embarrassed and if you do it wrong in front of people, you'll try your best to cover it up so no one will know what you've done.

However, this is the price you must pay if you want to achieve success. Let me ask you a question. When you first learnt to drive a car was it easy? Of course it wasn't, did you make loads of mistakes and stall the car and have kangaroo petrol all the time when you were learning to balance the clutch and accelerator? Did you know when to change gears? Did you know how to position your car in the right lane and when to indicate? Did you know how to parallel park?

Of course you didn't you learnt all of those skills bit by bit, didn't you? It involved hard work, dedication, not giving up and mastering all the skills that you needed to learn how to drive. This is the same with your Priceless Life Destination you must learn new skills which will very often involve hard work of mastering that new skill, but it's essential if you want to achieve your dreams.

Think of all the new skills you must learn to attain your dreams, use you pen as a magic wand again. Imagine you could be awesome at any particular skill, what would it be? If you could wave your magic wand and have any wish with regards to your new talents and skills, what would you wish for?

Whatever your answers are to the above questions will be your own individual answers to the skills and abilities you'll need to work on. Working on these skills will allow you to be the best you can be.

In other words you have to invest in you and what you do, learn everything about it, constantly keep dumping good stuff into your brain. Remember scientific tests prove that 80% of what we learn we forget the next day and the remaining 20% that's left we miss remember 10% of that. So it's only 10% that we actually remember, it's so important to keep continuously learning new empowering ideas and strategies. Set yourself a goal to become a lifelong learner, it's often said that the biggest learners are the biggest earners.

Learn To Earn

Here's my principles to learning and mastering any new skill, best of all it's easy and quick to apply and works all of the time, every time.

- Read in the area that you lack that skill, it could be books, magazines even if it's only 10-20 minutes a day. The more you read the more confident you'll become and be able to communicate better with yourself and others. I know it sounds simple but it's true.
- Listen to as much personal development audio programs as you can, listen to them in the car on your i- pod while you're running or at the gym. Transform your driving and exercise time into learning time.
- Attend seminars, workshops, mastermind or mentoring groups. So many peoples lives have transformed by

attending seminars simply by learning one key strategy that's changed their lives forever.

- Practise, practise, practise whatever you've learned, do it straight away because if you don't the longer you leave it, you'll never do it. Every time you hear a good idea instantly take action on it

Practise Makes Perfect

The more you practice what you are learning, the faster you will become competent and skilled in that area. The more you practice, the more confidence you will develop. The more you practice, the more rapidly you will overcome your feelings of inadequacy in that skill and the faster you will master it. The more you practice, the more rapidly you will add that skill to your mental toolbox where you will possess it for the rest of your life.

The Stages of Learning & Change

The secret we are after or the secret we all strive for is unconsciously competent, what does that mean? it means when we know what to do without even thinking about it and we just do it automatically. Let me explain, when you first learnt to drive your car you knew nothing about what to do or how to do it, Right?

You were what we call unconsciously incompetent or in other words you knew nothing and didn't know how to do it and hadn't a clue of where or how to start.

Then you got a little bit better and started to improve and you became consciously incompetent. This means you still know nothing about it but you know what to do. Or in other words you don't know how to drive a car but you know you must change gears to make it move.

Then you became consciously competent which means you started to get really good but you still had to think about what you did and when. You still had to remember when to change gear.

Then you became unconsciously competent this means you don't have to think about how or when to change gear you just do it automatically, you instantly know when to indicate and you just know when to change gear and which is the right gear to change to.

I see the learning and change process like this.

When you first start something new it seems impossible, then when you practise for a while, what's impossible soon becomes hard to do. With a little hard work what's hard to do becomes easy and then with dedication and motivation, what's easy becomes automatic.

I want you to read the above paragraph again and again and look at all different areas of your life where you've already applied this in your life. When you do this and associate yourself with it, a change will begin to occur in you. You'll realise that you have in the past and will be able to in the future develop new horizons and opportunities for yourself.

Let me ask you a question, when was the last time you were driving you thought about when to change gear? Never right, that's because you do it automatically but remember once it was impossible for you to do. You knew nothing about how to drive and it was a daunting and scary task. However you watched everybody else do it and said to yourself "*if they can do it, so can I.*" This is a success principle you must not forget.

CHAPTER NINE

The Naysayers and The Yaysayers

Choose your peer group wisely, because what they say and when they say it will infect your brain like a virus.

Craig Price

It's often been said that our life is always down to relationships, everything that you achieve, attain or fail at, is some way or another connected with others in some way shape or form. Your skill to find the right people at the right time in your life is critical.

The more people you know that can help you the better. They will if the opportunity is right place and at the right time, open doors for you that you could never have imagined and it can change your life and save you years in the process.

Nobody Can Do It On Their Own

A critical principle is for you to identify people, groups, and organisations or clubs whose help will get you towards your goal. This may sound a bit selfish but we all need some help so why not make it a mission of yours to actively seek out people who can help you.

Ask Yourself, Who Are The People I Need In My Life To Help Me

There are three types of people you'll need help from; these are people in and around your work, your family and friends. People in clubs and groups and organisations and you must make it your mission to develop relationships with them so they can help you. To do this you must form a strategy and work proactively and effectively to make this happen.

Make a list of the people at work that could help you, don't just limit the list to people who you just work with, remember they have friends. It could even be the customers and remember they have friends too. It could even be suppliers or other businesses you have relationships with. Out of all these people who or which have the greater ability to help you attain your Priceless Life Destination.

Remember if they are going to help you then you'll have to do something for them, be nice give something back for them personally. Look for every opportunity to help people at work and just simply do nice things for people and it will come back to you. I promise there is no way it cannot. Try your best at every opportunity to help in some way and best of all, do it when people least expect it.

The most popular people are those who will always lend a helping hand to others. The more people that like you support you and respect you, the more you will get paid and the faster you'll reach your Priceless Life Destination.

Develop a reputation as a positive, happy person, because those are the types of people we all love to be around don't we? Open your mind to new ways and resources and new ideas of how you can give value to the people around you and when you need them for help and support, they'll help you.

In business the most successful executives are the ones who network regularly and continuously expand their business and their network of other business people. They are always adding to their professional contact list.

Check out some of your local businesses in your area that may be beneficial to you and select and choose meetings they might attend and introduce yourself to them. Choose a club or regular meeting that you can volunteer your time, this will give you the chance to meet with and perform before other people who can help you in the future. Always remember the more doors of opportunity you knock on the more chances you have of them opening for you.

Make notes of certain people in newspapers in certain areas of business, remember their names and job titles then seek them out, because if you don't they will definitely not seek you out. Send them an email or a letter but it has to be something that is not business related find something that's of interest to them based on what you've read about them in the newspapers.

Each time you see a reason to talk to someone drop them a note or an email, befriend them on face book so they will see what you do. Remember a lot of the time I don't get through to see the right person but I know the more I try, the more I'll triumph. Even if you don't get through that time eventually you will meet them and next thing you know they'll remember that you sent them something and you'll be able to schedule a meeting with them.

Associate With The Right People

When I was a kid I had it drummed into me by my parents to always hang around with the good kids. I was told constantly not to hang around with the kids who were cheeky to their elders or teachers or who stole sweets from the local sweet shop. Why?

Because my parents knew that they would entice me to do the same. Why do the majority of children start smoking? All because they were enticed or bullied into it by other kids because they wouldn't be cool like them.

Essentially they copied them; they copied their behaviours and actions. My parents just like other parents knew this and this is so important in your adult life to hang around with the right people.

Make it a goal to hang around the right type of people, people that you admire, respect and look up to. But more importantly people who you would like to be like, so you can learn from them. Find positive goal oriented, future thinking people that want to do something with their lives and these people will charge you forward for success.

Rather than people who always argue for their own limitations and have an excuse for why their life is so crap.

Hanging around with the right type of people who are successful, motivated, determined and have a go getters attitude will take your life to next level quicker than you could ever imagine before.

If you play a sport with people who are worse than you, they'll bring you down to their level. Why? Because you stop trying you don't give it your all. When you know people aren't as good as you, your Dominating Delusional Destructive Dragon your subconscious mind takes over and tells you not to try. There are millions of examples in all different areas from sports to people's careers to business, where an average person obtaining average results, earning an average pay has super charged his career and his earning potential by working with new colleagues who are highly productive and future orientated .

When you continually associate, hang around with; listen to goal focused, future thinking, optimistic and go getting type of people an average person will perform at new levels of greatness. This is why almost every level of change in your life will have associations with the new people you hang around with in your life.

Remember just as it can change for the better, it can have the reverse effect. If you start to hang around with people who have an excuse for everything, who constantly tell you how bad it is for them. How they never seem to make things work for them or they've never had the right breaks in life, aren't lucky like everyone who's successful. Then you will almost certainly become like them and will take on their points of view and opinions in life.

If You Lie With Dogs, You'll Get Fleas

We all have points in our lives where we need people and when this happens there's always someone saying to you come this way, this is what you want to be doing. It's as if there's always someone opening a door or closing a door and guiding you in one way or another.

Think about the person you take advice from; are they an expert in their field? If they aren't don't listen to them. I see so many people who are overweight going to diet classes taught by an overweight person, why do these people take advice from people who obviously can't do it themselves? Only take advice from people who are successful in their field, only an idiot would take wealth management advice from a homeless person or weight loss advice from an overweight person wouldn't they?

I must spell this out for you so you've got it right. If you want to be become successful and you are really serious about it then you cannot waste time and effort with people who are going nowhere in their lives. I don't care how nice they are. I know this sounds really selfish and nasty but if you don't, these people will drag you down to their level. You must set high standards for your friends and associates and refuse to compromise or regret it at your peril.

So many people get into bad relationships and form friends with people that will never be able to help them. This is normal behaviour when we are younger, making mistakes is normal especially when you're young and don't know any better. However there is no excuse to stay in a situation that just keeps holding you back and the choice of people you hang around with on a regular basis has a massive impact on the behaviours and actions you'll have in the present and the future.

There are three types of people and I'll show you who to hang around with and who to avoid.

1. The Dream Stealer, this person must be avoided at all costs. How do you know what a Dream Stealer is? Their conversations are dull and always negative their main aim is to be an energy vampire. They will always without a shadow of a doubt tell you not to go for your goals. They'll tell you that it's too tough and only people who have been born with a silver spoon in their mouths, can become successful. They will come up with a million and one excuses of why they aren't successful, listen out for these excuses this is the tell tale sign of the dream stealer. Everywhere you go you will meet the dream stealer.

2. The Cheerleader, this person is someone who will encourage you, they are fun to be around, and they tell you how awesome you are. They will agree with your point of view, they will always hang onto your every word. However they don't really inspire you or make you feel like your full of energy or don't have many new and exciting ideas. (They are good to hang around and great people to know)

3. The Sparkler, this person is a must to have as a friend; they will always be working on their goals and their lives. They are always looking for new areas to improve their lives. They are successful and creative. They will share their ideas with you; they have endless energy and are such a joy to be around. They boost your energy levels and make you feel great about yourself. However there is a challenge, there simply aren't many sparklers around. When you find a sparkler hang out with them and hang on to them and learn everything you can from them.

The Naysayers and The Yaysayers

- Make a list of people in your work environment, personal life and clubs or organisations.
- Develop a plan to help them in some way shape or form.
- Make a list of the top people in your area and make a plan to get to know them personally.
- Look for each and every opportunity to expand your relationship circles of business and in your community and send them letters, emails join them on face book or twitter.
- Avoid the Dream Stealers
- Find the Cheerleaders.
- Learn from the Sparklers and hang out with and hold onto them.

CHAPTER TEN

Flexible People Never Get Bent Out Of Shape

If you don't get in the know you will never get in the now

Craig Price

This one quality to remain flexible in pursuit of your goals is a fundamental trait if you want to be, do and have more than you could have dreamed about before.

We see it everyday in all areas of our lives some people will have happier lives, make more money, obtain greater skills and create abundance in their lives compared to others. Flexibility means the quality of being adaptable or variable. If you can be adaptable in life your life will change for the better so much faster.

When you're flexible you enter the world with an open mind and can adapt in any situation like an automatic reflex action. This will instantly take you and your life forward to your Priceless Life Destination. Acquiring the quality of flexibility will undoubtedly sky rocket you to your goals faster than the average person.

When you are rigid or reluctant to change and you also fear change like a lot of people do. You can't make that certain shift in your life that's needed to move your life forward. You just seem to stick in the same old rut, doing what you've always done and obtaining the same old results.

Each and everyday things are changing around us, change is automatic and inevitable, however if you don't get in the know you can never get in the now. Change is everywhere and comes to us all from all different areas of our lives, so much so that it's almost impossible to know what may happen next.

Change is like a monster that's out of control and quite often our best laid plans have to be scrapped the very next day as a result of a completely new and unpredictable occurrence that has headed our way. When this happens we must remain flexible in our approach and our thinking and our new plans.

Change Can Equal Stress

Tests have shown that people dislike change in their lives, they don't like or enjoy their routine to be disrupted. One of the greatest causes in the world today for stress and anxiety is a change of circumstances. When successful people encounter a change in their lives they do things differently. They move fast and take action by firstly asking themselves a better question. *"With this new change that's now present in my life, is what I'm doing working or not."* If it's not you must be flexible. The only way you will know if what you are doing is working, is to ask yourself that question. This question is something you must continually be asking yourself.

The only way if you know, if what you're doing is working and getting you closer to your Price Life Destination, is to constantly ask yourself the question "Is what I'm doing, working or not?"

Become Open To New Ideas In Your Life

To stay in the flexible zone you must always remain open to new ideas. It's been said on numerous occasions that just one simple idea has made people millions. Just one idea can change your life forever, it can lead you to your dream lifestyle or it can lead you down the pathway to doom and gloom.

Remember I said that the biggest earners are the biggest learner's. Well it's true you must read everything you can on your chosen subject. Listen to audio programs and attend seminars constantly always be upgrading you and your mind with the latest technologies.

Remember if you're not in the know you're not in the now

Whoever learns the most and remembers the information will always have the power over someone who doesn't take the time and effort to learn. Ignorance is not an excuse; the information is everywhere if you're willing to seek it out.

Just think of change like a television

When you've just bought a brand new state of the art television, mobile phone or computer how long does it take until a new and improved version comes out? How long will it be until your appliance you bought is no longer their most recent invention?

Probably about six month's right? This is just like life, if you're not constantly on the lookout for new stuff and ideas to improve upon. You'll be stuck in the past wondering what happened and why. Electrical manufacturers are constantly developing new and improved equipment to make our lives easier. If you're not looking at new ways to constantly improve or to replace your products with something better. You can guarantee that someone else will be staying up all night thinking of new ways to do it and you'll be left behind.

How often do we see an advert on television showing you the latest gadgets and how it will improve our lives and make things much easier for us? Then what happens, a few weeks down the line another manufacturer has developed a new and improved product that will do so much more and quicker.

It's been said time and time again that life is a constant battle to overcome problems; if you haven't got any problems then you must be dead. It really is as simple as that, all of us have problems or challenges in our lives. Only when you're flexible can you overcome these problems.

You Must Be Clear About Your Goal, But You Must Be Flexible About Achieving It.

We've all heard the saying, "*as one door closes another door opens.*" Well this is so true. When you are flexible and fully aware and open to new flexibilities and opportunities in your life, you'll begin to move forward in the right direction.

Within every problem lies a solution, start thinking like an optimist. A pessimist is one who makes difficulties of his opportunities and an optimist is one who makes opportunities of his difficulties. When you start on your own journey you will without a shadow of a doubt, hit a roadblock that stops you. When this happens you must stop revaluate and look for another door of opportunity. I promise you it's always there hiding in the most unexpected places.

When you are flexible you'll automatically and quickly take advantage of that new opportunity and you'll quickly start to progress forward. The inevitable will happen again; you'll hit another roadblock that stops you. Just as before you must find a way, another doorway will open for you. You just have to train yourself to look for it and stop living in the past saying to yourself "*why does this always happen to me. Every time I take two steps forward, I take one step back.*" This is life, get over it instantly and stop dwelling over it and continuously keep moving forward in the direction of your Priceless Life Destination.

This may happens to you on numerous occasions. In almost every case you will most definitely achieve your best successes and personal achievements, completely different from what you thought it would have originally looked like. The secret ingredient is to remain flexible at all times.

New possibilities and endless opportunities are attracting their way to you everyday and in every way, you've just got to open your eyes to it. Remember our subconscious minds only see what we allow it to see. How many times have you gone to the cupboard to find a jar and you've not seen it anywhere and then someone comes right behind you and says *"look it's right here, it's under your nose."* It's as if you couldn't see it, but it was always there staring you in the face. This was because while you were looking for it you were constantly saying to yourself *"I can't see it, I can't see it anywhere."*

Which is exactly right, whatever you say to yourself will become your reality. So start opening up your mind to all the opportunities that are out there, just waiting to be grabbed. Remember there is always a way if you look hard enough, the more you look the more your subconscious mind will become creative and will find a new way.

Remember it's important to aim to be flexible and open, there is always another way to attain your goal, no matter what happens. Your number one goal must be to stay focused, alert and aware to what that new way might be. Once you've found it take action in that new direction as fast as you can, this will empower you and allow you to reach your goal. Sometimes this can be in the most unexpected and surprising ways that you could ever imagine.

Remember what the job of the Dominating, Delusional, Destructive Dragon is, its job is to keep you safe, to keep you in the realms of normality for you. It keeps you in the same old, same old, it hates change. Why? Because it knows that when change happens you have to enter the unknown and it's afraid of the unknown. The Triple D Dragon lives in the past and tells you it didn't work last time, so why try it this time.

Remember you are attracted to certain types of people that you feel comfortable with. There are certain people that you are happy to be around because of all the programming that the Triple D Dragon has had in the past. This is more often than not a direct reflection of the people that your parents or any powerful person in your life, told you was acceptable to associate with when you were younger.

Start to open and broaden your horizons. People who you don't feel comfortable with may just be the doorway that you've been looking for. It could be that you've just not seen it in the correct light before. Start to look in different areas, different ways, different people and different signs along the way that will take you to you Priceless Life Destination.

Look at everything as if you were seeing it for the first time with no preconceived ideas and you will move in the right direction.

Flexible People Never Get Bent Out Of Shape

- Always ask yourself the question "Is what I'm currently doing, working or not"
- See Life as it really is, full of roadblocks in our way.
- Make new decisions quickly when a door closes.
- Open your eyes to the signs along the way.
- Remember it's not always the way you thought it would be.
- Change is automatic and it must be for you.

CHAPTER ELEVEN

Your Action Plan

Actions speak louder than words but not nearly as often.

Mark Twain

The only way for your goals to become reality, is to set in place a plan and stick to it everyday. There is no skill that comes anywhere near to attaining your true potential and achieving your own Priceless Life, than making a plan of action.

Every single thing that you have achieved in your life up to this present moment and every single thing that you will ever achieve in the future will involve a plan. Each and every achievement you've ever attained has a multitude of tiny steps along the way to get you to your destination.

Even something as simple as making a pie has to have a set plan of how to create it. Each pie must have a recipe of ingredients and a method and a plan of how to create it. When you can acquire this procedure of little steps to reach your destination, you will accomplish far more than the average person who wanders aimlessly through life without a plan.

The number one aim of setting a plan of action is to break down your journey or your goal into small tasks, with precise deadlines of when to accomplish them by. This is an easy skill to master with practise. Just like everything else the more you practise it, the better you will get at it.

Putting It All Together

We've already gone over some of the secret ingredients of the Priceless Success Principles and by following these principles you will guarantee your own success.

- You must know what you want, your goal or Priceless Life Destination.
- You have written them out or *"think in ink"* as I like to call it.
- You must know why you want it all the reasons why, as they are your motivating factor.
- You have organised them by priority.
- You have set deadlines to achieve them by.
- You have identified which new skills you need and more importantly you've started to learn them.
- You have identified that you can't do it on your own and you've noticed which people, groups or clubs can help you.
- You've slayed The Dominating Delusional Destructive Dragon.

Now is the time to put it all together in an action plan. All people who have achieved greatness in their lives have worked from written plans. When you watch your favourite film the actors have worked to a script which is just like a plan.

The tallest skyscrapers in the world to the small one bedroom bungalows were all carefully designed and thought out all in advance from the beginning to the end. Could you imagine a builder starting to build a house without a plan, he wouldn't know where to start and that is exactly the same with your life.

Plans are critical for success, it's said that people work best when they follow a plan as they feel they have a clear route to their destination. Anyone who says they don't have the time to plan will almost definitely make silly mistakes, waste lots of precious time and lose lots of money and energy.

These are my principles for creating your plan for awesomeness

When you get in the planning zone and start planning your Priceless Life Destination, your subconscious mind starts thinking of new ways and ideas of how to tackle the challenges that you face.

The second principle that happens is, you start thinking about what you have to do to attain your Priceless Life Destination and this will save you time, money, energy and effort.

The third principle that happens is, when you set a plan you can see the stuff that you will do wrong and it helps you to avoid making stupid and silly mistakes. You will start to say to yourself *"What could happen if I did this or did that"*

It is so important to spend time in the planning stage and just do some really careful thinking of what your own individual steps are to attain your desires.

The fourth principle helps you to see your strengths and your opportunities that you can so easily take advantage of. These opportunities wouldn't have been apparent if you wouldn't have made a plan.

The fifth principle of planning is it helps you to focus your time wisely and to concentrate on one thing at a time, this way you'll just get stuff done. If your focus is everywhere we all know what happens, we achieve nothing we seem to be busy all day but get nothing done.

A plan is quite simply a list of what you need to do from the beginning all the way to the end. The proper process of planning is to organise your list by priority and order of sequence. It's really simple, firstly figure out which tasks are more important than others. Then just organise the list and start with the first step.

Remember that no plan is perfect

When you first set a plan don't expect to get it right straight away, this is a new concept for you. Just keep checking in with your plan and yourself everyday and keep asking yourself *"Is this working or not?"*

We've all heard the saying *"let's go back to the basics,"* well keep doing it, constantly go back and see if it's working.

For some reason it seems that when you begin to start work on your goals you always have setbacks, difficulties seem to just appear. This is totally normal, it takes dedication, hard work and lots of effort to become successful.

This is the price you must pay to achieve your Priceless Life Destination.

Set yourself little steps

To achieve each goal it seems daunting until you break it into small steps, break it down to the first step. If this step requires a list of steps to achieve it then you haven't broken it down enough, the first step is the first step and that's it.

Decide what the first step is and just do it. Then continue until you've reached your goal or Priceless Life Destination. Remember each goal has little steps all along the way until you reach your desired outcome. Once you finish 1 step, identify the next step, identify it and *DO IT* and so on and so on until you reach your first Bench Mark or Goal.

As soon as you reach your first bench mark or goal it's time to figure out the first step on the journey to the next bench mark or goal and so on.

Ask yourself everyday *"what's my next step"*

Use the form to help break down the steps.

Breaking Down Your Goal Into Little Steps

Remember if you don't
Think in ink it won't happen

Remember to ask yourself what's my next step?
Remember to break it Down To the First Step, if this step
requires a list of steps you've not broken it down enough.

The first step is the first step & that's it.

Step 1.

_____
_____
_____
_____
_____
_____
_____
_____

Step 2.

_____
_____
_____
_____
_____
_____
_____

Step 3.

_____

_____

_____

_____

_____

_____

_____

_____

Step 4.

_____

_____

_____

_____

_____

_____

_____

Step 5.

_____

_____

_____

_____

_____

_____

_____

Step 6.

_____
_____
_____
_____
_____
_____
_____
_____

Your Action Plan

- Make a list of everything that you must do, leave nothing out.
- Organise your list by sequence of small steps,
- Organise your list by priority, if this step requires a list of steps you've not broken it down enough the first step is the first step and that's it.
- Everyday ask yourself *"what's my next step."*

CHAPTER TWELVE

Get Organised

*If you don't start managing time, then time will almost
Definitely manage you & your life*

Craig Price

Keeping your time under control is so important to success, how many times have you said, *"I don't have enough time in the day to do everything."*

Controlling time is another skill you can learn. I don't care how disorganised you think you are, or how much you've always put stuff off until tomorrow or have got caught up in time wasting jobs. You can become a master at controlling time in your life. With consistent practise you can become so much more effective and efficient and be able to cram in much more stuff into your day.

Becoming organised is a true friend of becoming successful. To control your own individual time, firstly you must know your goals. Organise them into priority and be absolutely 100% clear of what is the most important thing for you to do at any given time in your day.

You must set aside time for all different areas of your life from work, health and fitness, financial, careers and relationships. For each and every area you must zone in on the highest priority at that moment in time for what you must accomplish that day. Rather than trying to do everything all day and get nothing done.

You must set yourself a standard of what is high priority and medium priority and low priority for you that day.

Once you've figured out how you're going to become wealthy, it's time to organise yourself. In order to get there in the shortest time possible, you have to strategise. If you're working with others, make a list of how many people are involved and their various job functions and what you'll need them to do.

Clear all the clutter; establish a day-to-day routine that takes you forward. Once you're used to the work that you're doing, it won't be as hard to continue doing it.

Remember that the beginning is most often the hardest part. If you can survive the initial plunge towards success, you can prove to yourself that you can get all the way there.

When you start to exercise, the first two or three weeks are always the hardest because your body aches and you'll have pains in your body that you never thought was pos-sible. Once you've committed yourself and you've broken through the pain barrier of those first few weeks, will you start to see the results and you'll become successful. I use a saying with my clients *"if it doesn't hurt, then it doesn't work."* Remember this and constantly go in the direction of the things that you don't want to do, this will guarantee your own individual success.

Stop doing all the time stealing things that take up your day. We all waste time everyday, notice where and what areas you waste time and organise a set amount of time each day to work on your personal development.

Do you often find that time runs away with you all day long? Do you find that you seem to be doing lots and lots of things, but never seem to get the things done that you need to?

I know this is a challenge for a lot of people, well there are two things that you can do. The first is to have an hour less sleep every day and by the end of the week you will have gained seven hours in a week. Just think seven hours more in a week, just by taking an extra hour less sleep a day.

We all waste time by watching stuff on television we don't really want to watch or by doing things that just take our time away from us. Below you'll find my proven way of gaining more time so easily and efficiently. It all starts with prioritising your time and just like you would set an appointment with a client make an appointment with yourself for a specific time in the day and stick to it.

"The most valuable commodity I know is time, don't waste it."

Use the form every day to help you get the important stuff done

The Priceless Time Plan

What Are Your Most Important
Things To Accomplish Today?
Put Them In Order Of Their
Importance.

Only Do Number 2 When You've
Completed Number 1.

1. _____

   _____

2. _____

   _____

3. _____

   _____

4. _____

   _____

5. _____

   _____

6. _____

   _____

Plan Your Day Using The Time Slots

The Most Valuable Commodity I
Know Is Time, Don't Waste It.
Make That Appointment With
Yourself NOW!

7.00 _____
7.30 _____
8.00 _____
8.30 _____
9.00 _____
9.30 _____
10.00 _____
10.30 _____
11.00 _____
11.30 _____
12.00 _____
12.30 _____
1.00 _____
1.30 _____
2.00 _____
2.30 _____
3.00 _____
3.30 _____
4.00 _____
4.30 _____
5.00 _____
5.30 _____
6.00 _____
6.30 _____
7.00 _____

Create time zones for yourself

Plan your day into small time zones of 30 minutes, 60 minutes and 90 minute zones of totally uninterrupted time, just for you to accomplish the things you need to that day. These time zones are so important for your attainment of any goal.

Obviously an easy way is to rise early in the morning and work non-stop without any interruptions. The steps or goals you set for yourself often need that long time scale, with single minded focus and concentration to get the job done.

Remember whether you work for someone or you don't, each time you go to work you are being paid to work for a specific period of time to achieve a specific result. If you didn't get all your work done in the day you would have your boss chasing you, this must be how you see your organising on your goals.

Start to become results orientated and always ask yourself the question *"what would be the best use of my time now."*

If you ever feel yourself slowing down or feel yourself going into the *putting it off until tomorrow mode,* just repeat to yourself a phrase I tell my clients *"if it doesn't hurt, it doesn't work"* it's only the stuff that's going to hurt you or put you out of your comfort zone or cause you some inconvenience that will help you become successful. Remember that so called pain or uncomfortable feeling, only lasts for a few moments the pride of actually getting it done lasts forever.

The Priceless Time Plan

Take 10 minutes to make a list of the six things you must do the night before for the next day. Then place them in order of importance

Successful people make a habit of doing things in their order of importance. *Why?*

Because if they didn't, they would get bogged down with all the time consuming stuff we all get bogged down with everyday.

Use The Priceless Time Plan to help you get stuff done. An awesome tip is once you've done number 1 re-prioritise your list again, because sometimes number 3 could be more important than number 2. So always check and re-prioritise if necessary.

When it comes to time we must follow the "Priceless P Principle"

- Protect your time,
  Don't let anything or anyone distract you. Turn off your phone and your emails, turn of twitter and face book.

- Preserve
  Preserve your our time, time is the only thing we all have in common. We all have 24 hours a day, so preserve yours. As I said before the most valuable commodity I know is time, don't waste it.

- Prioritise
  Prioritise your time wisely and schedule what you are going to do and when. Constantly ask yourself which task is the most important in order of importance from one through to six.

- Plan.
  Successful people plan their day the night before. Take 10 minutes the night before and fill in the form. Write down the six things you need to do in order of their importance. Set a time slot for each and only do number 2 when you've completed number 1 Only do number 3 when you've

completed number 2. Once you've completed a task tick it off.

"As With All Great Ideas, This Is Simple. Take This Challenge, It's Worth The Effort, I promise"

CHAPTER THIRTEEN

The "M" Word

Strength does not come from winning. Your struggles develop your strengths. When you go through hardships and decide not to surrender, that is strength

Arnold Schwarzenegger

One of the most important aspects of being and becoming successful is maintaining motivation. To stay motivated you must refresh your motivators daily, you must find something that motivates you. It could be a song a film a motivational quote an activity, anything that will get you back on track when you don't feel very motivated.

Having the motivation to continue is huge. Most people who make it to the action phase start taking action, but stop when they don't experience immediate results. Do everything in your power to maintain your drive to succeed.

When you have a grand goal, it can be tempting to give up and claim that you're goal was impossible in the first place. However, there are plenty of people in the world who are living proof that you are rewarded when you work hard and smart.

Maintaining motivation and to follow through on your goals is back to the "why's" of your Priceless Life Destination. Once you've found enough reasons or why's for attaining your Priceless Life Destination, you'll always follow through to the end and achieve your goal.

The "<u>why's</u>" or reasons of why you want your goal have to be so strong for you that you focus on them everyday.

Each and everyday ask yourself the following questions

What will it do for me attaining my goal?

What will it give me?

What will it mean for me?

Your reasons for attaining your goal must be so powerful that every time you think of it, you want it more and more each day.

Just as everyone is different we all have different ways to motivate ourselves. You must find what works for you best, I find this just works for me. I love to watch films that inspire me and I listen to songs that move me and change my state. I watch Rocky 3 over and over again. Especially the part where Rocky has lost his mojo and he starts training with Apollo Creed, but he just can't seem to get his head in gear. It's as if he's holding onto something that just keeps stopping him from being the champion again. It's only when his wife Adrianne gets to the main reason why he's acting and behaving like he is, that he can let it all go.

I find that watching that part of the film first thing in the morning and last thing at night works the best for me. I put it on loop and watch it again and again and again and each time I watch it and listen to the music. I allow the music and the words of the actors to motivate me for the day ahead.

Our subconscious minds are always working and communicating with us all day long. Have you ever noticed when you watch a horror film before you go to bed, it gives you nightmares? Your subconscious mind is continuously going over the film you've just watched and you're listening out for every noise in the night. Thinking to yourself that it's the axe man and he's going to get you.

The same thing happens when you watch films that are meaningful and powerful for you before you go to sleep. It works the same way but your subconscious mind is focussing on the powerful film and the feelings you associated with it. Whilst you're asleep your mind is constantly and persistently concentrating on those great feelings and associations you felt. It starts programming your mind in a different more beneficial and empowering way so you'll accomplish your dreams faster.

CHAPTER FOURTEEN

Think About It

Your imagination is the preview of life's coming attractions

Albert Einstein

It's said that we only use 5% of our brains capacity, yet we have at our disposal our very own unlimited powers to create our own destiny by thinking about it. This is why the average person fails in their attainment of their goals or dreams they have for themselves or their family and at best only achieve average results.

The majority of people don't harness the greatest power that you possess in the world, your subconscious mind. For so long throughout history people just take it for granted, or don't become aware of its awesome abilities to transform their lives. People who master this concept will often achieve more in one or two years than the average person could achieve in their whole lifetime.

When you become a master of your mind or your Dominating Delusional Destructive Dragon, you will without a shadow of a doubt move quicker towards your goals than you could ever imagine. Mastering the ability to imagine or visualise is possibly the greatest power you can possess. It's a fact your life will improve when your pictures you see inside your head improve. The pictures you hold in your head are a direct reflection of your life today, when you change the pictures you hold onto on the inside about yourself, your opportunities on the outside will change in accordance to your new pictures.

When you visualise or imagine you actually attract those ideas and pictures into your life. It works a bit like a magnet and the people, resources and connections that you need to attain your goals seem to just appear. Just as you become what you think about most of the time, you become what you visualise most of the time as well. The mental pictures that you regularly see become your very own reality. How do I know this? Let me ask you a question. If you saw, you and your very own circumstances different than you do today, would your life be in a completely different direction? Of course it would.

One of the traits of successful people is to imagine an ideal or dream like future for themselves. Leonardo Di Vinci imagined we could fly in planes years before it was ever possible. Everything in your life good or bad begins with a mental picture.

Too often I have clients who say they can't imagine or visualise their own future, remember every time you think of someone or something or remember an upcoming event or a just daydream guess what you are doing you are visualising. So you are already a professional at it, aren't you?

It is so important that you learn to harness this ability of your mind and spend your time each and every day, using this power to achieve the goals that are your utmost desires.

Successful people see inside their heads the success they want to enjoy in advance, they enjoy the experience by using past success's that are similar to the new goal or Priceless Life Destination. Think of a time in your life when you were doing something and it was brand new to you. Think of a time when you weren't 100% sure of how to do it, what did you do? You recalled a previous experience and used that vision or picture of what you did before to help you this time, didn't you?

Just as we have two Dragons inside our head, we also use visualisation to our failures as well. We watch the pictures the Triple D Dragon gives us when we failed and we recall and think about the previous failed experiences we had. Our Triple D dragon is always thinking of the last time we did it wrong or failed miserably, then we imagine ourselves failing again. We then go into that new experience the mind has automatically been programmed for failure and not success. Be careful how you visualise or think about past events as it will affect your future.

The way that you perform on the outside is a mirror reflection of your self image on the inside. Your self image you have is made up entirely of the pictures you hold onto inside your head before any event or circumstance that takes place. Just like you can choose which Dragon to listen to The Dominating Delusional Destructive Dragon or The Delightful Daring Dynamic Dragon. You have total control over which Dragon controls your pictures you see; you choose what you want in your life.

You can choose to see positive, inspiring and exciting images or you can spend all day thinking and seeing images of failure. The choice is yours.

Remember that virtually everything you have achieved or failed at in your life, is the work of which dragon you chose to let you see your mental pictures. If you look back on your life you'll find that almost everything you visualised came true, passing your driving test, buying your first house, finding your first love, going on holiday, finding a job, buying a certain pair of designer jeans all these things came true. For all of these to come true you would have had to see them in your head first.

Just as all the positive things came true, so did all the negative things in your life. Everyone uses this power each and everyday throughout their lives but far too often it's used in the wrong way. It's used in a way where it's as if you're on constant default of the Dominating Delusional Destructive Dragon. It's imperative that you take control of the visualisation or imagining process. Make sure that the images you see are only of the goals you want to attain and the person you want to be.

In other words you personally control the shaping process of your personality and characteristic traits by the mental pictures you allow which dragon to hold on to. If you change the way you see your pictures everyday and every hour and every minute then you will and must change the way you think, feel and act. This will in turn change the way people will react to you and obviously will change the way and direction of your life.

This idea isn't new, professional sports people have been doing it for years, Mohammed Ali did it before every fight He would say things like *"Archie Moor, you're going in four"* he called it future history. Out of the nineteen fights Mohammed Ali had, he predicted seventeen of the outcomes in the exact round by knock-out.

Ali saw himself performing at his best. Even before going into the ring to fight for hours he would visualise the run of events, from each round what he would do and how he would do it. He constantly visualised himself being the champion of the world over and over again. Each time he created this inside his head, he would associate himself with all the emotions which came with being the champion of the world. This had the effect and programming on Ali's brain that he had already won the fight.

What was Mohammed Ali's favourite saying? *"I am the greatest"* by saying this to himself he believed it to be true. Remember whatever we say to ourselves or think about we will attract into our lives.

Now remember, you don't have to close your eyes to imagine or visualise. All day long you are imagining or visualising and see-ing pictures inside your head, just think of all the times in the day when you go off to your own little land of your own imagination. I like to imagine or visualise when I'm running I find it's great for me, you'll know with practise what works best for you. It maybe that closing your eyes is best, play around with all different ways for yourself and see which way rocks your world.

The Principles To Priceless Visualisation

Following these principles will ensure your success, just practise and harness this awesome power because to be successful you've got to do this for the rest of your life.

Principle 1. The More The Better

The first principle is how many times a day you create your pic-tures of achieving your Priceless Life Destination. How many times you see yourself operating at an extraordinary level of success in an event or circumstance. The more the better the more times a day you see a clear mental picture of yourself doing what you need and must do, the quicker it will become reality.

Principle 2. The Longer The Better

The second principle is how long you can hold that picture in your minds eye of you being successful. The longer you can hold the images of success in your mind the quicker and deeper it will embed into your subconscious mind and the quicker it will appear in your life.

Principle 3. The Clearer The Better

The third principle is the clearer the better. When you see it crystal clear in full high definition and hear it in full surround sound or even in 3 dimensional images. Practise seeing it in the best possible way for you, so it's that clear you feel that you could touch it. Simply by doing this, the quicker it will be attracted into your life.

Principle 4. The More Emotions The Better

The fourth principle is harnessing the emotions and feelings you associate with your visualisation. This is the most important and powerful part of the whole process. If your feelings and emotions are so strong and powerful, you can often have your goal within a few days. Allow all those feelings each time you imagine your goal to fill your body and feel how awesome it feels when you've achieved your goal. Your body will soon get used to this awesome feeling and will program your subconscious to look out for every opportunity and possibility it can to get you there quicker than you can imagine.

One of the reasons or common mistakes people make when visualising is they fall into a trap of only visualising part of what they want. They only visualise one aspect of their goals or Priceless Life Destination, they simply miss out the big stuff. Or they will imagine something that makes them feel a certain way and that feeling won't be a part of their new reality they want to attract.

Let me explain what I mean, let's say you want to earn loads of money and you see yourself sitting at your kitchen table counting thousands and thousands of pounds. You see yourself putting all of the money in piles and feeling great about yourself for doing it. Let me ask you the question how times do you see people or have you heard about people who count thousands and thousands of pounds on the kitchen table? You don't do you; money gets paid directly into your bank account. You would be better off by visualising the money in your account, looking at your bank statement or visualising yourself paying a cheque into your bank.

Visualise areas of your life one at a time, each time you visualise you want to do it with creativity. Don't keep bringing up the same old image again and again, instead actively improve your visualisation slide into the image you've made of yourself and see it through your own eyes rather than watching it as if you were the director of the movie. Play around with it, see which way makes you feel stronger.

Experience the emotions you will achieve when you've reached your Priceless Life Destination. All you need to do for your visualisation to be realised into reality, is to ensure it is vivid, bright and intense. Make sure it's held within the focus of your mind and it's just yourself at the focus of your visualisation. In other words always see yourself experiencing it. Keep updating and improving it until you are satisfied that you have a strong idea of what you want yourself to be, do and have in the future.

As you watch your visualisation, envision the brilliant vibrant colours, hear the sounds, feel the emotions and sensations in your body. Even smell fragrances with your nose and tastes in your mouth. If a limiting thought enters your head simply breathe them in and let them go and laugh at them when they're leaving.

Some people call visualising rehearsing your dance moves to success, whatever you want to call it, just do it. If you don't you are simply turning yourself off from success. I promise if you do it, you'll thank me for it.

REMEMBER visualisation works both ways, whatever you imagine whether it's good or bad you'll attract into your life. If you only visualise once and that's it you may get something back in return, however if you do it often and make it part of your daily routine or ritual. I promise you that you will get what you wish for or visualise.

If you want to achieve something really significant for yourself, start creating it in your mind first. Work continuously with it until it becomes a compulsion and then it will become inevitable.

CHAPTER FIFTEEN

Do The Do Everyday

Nothing is impossible the word itself says "I'm possible"

Audrey Hepburn

Studies upon studies have concluded one unmistakeable commonality between successful business people, sports people, sales people, managers and top leaders in their field is the quality of taking action immediately on their goals.

Successful people are action orientated, they just move quicker than the average person, they just get stuff done. While the average person is thinking about it, the successful person is making it happen. They are busy people, they start earlier than the average person, they stay later than the average person and they are constantly in motion moving forward to their desired destination.

Unsuccessful people have tendencies to stay in bed and have an extra lie in, in the morning. They start at the very last moment and quit at the first moment they can. They tend to always want to take breaks; they tend to take time off work and seem to have a carefree attitude towards work.

Successful people will always go that extra mile and do that little bit more while the average person stops and says "*enough is enough, I'm done and that's it."* Often studies have shown that the most successful people in life are always doing more than they were paid for, they are always looking for different ways to contribute and in often cases they went miles beyond what was expected of them.

If you work for a company you must be willing to take on more responsibility than you are getting paid for. You must go that extra mile and impress the people who pay you, when you do this your world will change. Work on projects for your boss over the weekends and learn everything you can, constantly keep asking your boss for more responsibility.

Complete tasks quickly, professionally and extremely well. Don't delay in your tasks move quickly and efficiently and the people that pay your wages will notice you. When you ask someone for more responsibility, you'll be surprised what a positive impact you will make on them. Remember when you do get the responsibility you want, you must complete the task quickly. Very quickly you'll be known as the go to guy and you'll start moving up the ladder quicker than you can imagine.

Remember this, we all know how quickly time flies by don't we. A year can go by so quickly and when you've argued for your limitations you'll find it's been another year full of "*what if's and maybe's*." You've got to use this time wisely if you don't this time next year you'll be where you don't want to be. Living where you don't want to live, driving what you don't want to drive and being the person you don't want to be. The time to change is now, if you don't, another year will pass by quicker than the year before and you'll wonder where it went. Remember that the time is going to pass by anyway, so you may as well get the most out of it as you can.

Start a little earlier every day, work a little later every day, start by doing it bit by bit and set your alarm 5 minutes earlier once a week. At the end of three months you've saved an hour a month. Or if you're like me, just go for it and do it. Make a decision and set your alarm an hour earlier every morning

Doing The Do

Momentum is the key to improvement, this principle of maintaining momentum is awesome, once you're moving you stay moving. The only challenge is you've got to start, remember It's the emotion that creates the motion, so take a check in with the Triple D Dragon. Once you're moving it's easy to keep going. Successful people are constantly moving all the time; they are working on themselves and their goals. Momentum means you get up early and keep going all day long. Get into that habit of staying in the zone of momentum.

We all know our lives are a direct representation of what we put into it, if you want more, you have to do more. Average people tend to have a saying that goes something like this *"I'll catch up in the afternoon."* They find it very easy to waste the hours of the day and they think and feel they will catch up later on in the day or later on in the week.

When we start to move we continue to move, as it's so much easier to. Let me explain when you eat a chocolate biscuit do you just have one? No of course you don't do you? You have two or three or sometimes the whole pack. When you start you keep going, so do things everyday to keep you moving towards your dreams. Do things quickly and work with a sense of urgency for the day. If you complete a task quicker than you expected don't just sit around, start the next task.

Imagine that it's your tax return deadline date, you'll do anything to get that document in on time to avoid a penalty and a fine. Do the same with your daily tasks work on them as if you will incur a penalty for your life.

Make that decision to get up earlier in the morning, become more productive in your days. Start immediately when you wake up, these simple additions to your life will supercharge you to your own greatness and something that once seemed like hard work will be achievable.

Take time each day to investigate with yourself of why you are just not doing it. Ask yourself the question *"why am I not doing it."* If there was a time in your life when you were the person you've always wanted to be and you were getting the results you always wanted to have, ask yourself *"what am I not doing now, that I was doing when I was the person I want to be again?"* Then just do it.

Without a shadow of a doubt one of the key principles of most successful people is they make a decision to not just be alright at something. They make a decision to be awesome at what they do. They make a decision that at whatever cost, whether it will be financially or time consuming they will pay any sacrifice necessary to become successful.

These people make a decision to be the best they can possibly be in their chosen field or industry. This decision to do this moves them quicker and farther away from any other average person and sky rockets them to a different place to earn substantially more amounts of money than they could have possibly imagined previously.

I see so many people walking around with an attitude that if they did something right then it was a one off or just a flash in the pan. So many people see themselves just as an average person its scary, if someone does something really well then they don't want to tell anyone about it. Why? Because it sounds like bragging and nobody likes a bragger or they will just think they've been lucky and never give themselves full recognition for their achievements.

This is something you must put right immediately, because if you don't you'll hang on to this mindset forever. One of the key principles I learned was that everyone even the best professionals in the world were at one time in their lives an amateur every winner was once a beginner. Or in other words everyone who is good at something today was once really lousy at it and all they did was learn how to do it. If someone else has learned it then so can you, what I quickly learned was this is true for everything and everybody in life, this is the mind set you must adopt instantly to become successful.

Remember that no one and I mean no one is better than you are. All that's happened is they've dedicated time, effort and energy to learn something that you haven't been bothered about previously and that's it. When you totally realise this, your life will change. Please read the last paragraph again and again until it really sinks inside your subconscious mind so you can see it and accept it for what it is. *THE TRUTH.*

Remember everything in life and I mean everything is learnable. You can learn anything and you must continue to learn new ways to become successful and improve yourself in all areas of your life. If you're not confident speaking in front of other people learn it, like I've said everything is learnable. The only reason someone is doing better in any area of their life than you, is because you have simply not learned those skills that they have.

There are no limits to what you can learn, which means there is no limits on what you can accomplish, doesn't it? The only limits are the ones that you constantly place on yourself and store in your subconscious mind and the Triple D Dragon tells you not to even try it. These self limitations are only because you haven't learnt that particular skill yet and that is it, nothing else.

It makes sense that once you've learned that skill you'll become unstoppable. The only thing that can stop you from learning this new skill is you. So get out of the way of yourself from learning and soak up as much awesome stuff that you can. This principle of learning new techniques or ideas will take you to your Priceless Life Destination.

Will learning be easy? Let me think, of course it won't. Anything worth having takes time, dedication, commitment and hard work, but if you want it and I mean really want it and you're willing to commit to it and go the distance. Then it is worth every single bit of effort that you have to apply to it. Look, if it wasn't for studying or learning would we have doctors? No we wouldn't. But they dedicate themselves to life long learning to help people and you must do the same.

I'll share this with you later on in the book, but to achieve a new project or attain a new goal you must become a different person. When you learn new things and apply it into your life you become a different person instantly and tasks that once were impossible become possible. When you've learnt that new skill that you must learn to get you to where you want to go, you will become someone that you never thought you could be.

One of the greatest secret ingredients all successful people have is the ability to learn new stuff and apply it instantly into their lives. Far too often people feel that because they didn't do well at school they are destined to do the same throughout their lives. This truly limits their own individual success.

I see lots of clients who hang on to this belief that they had when they were younger. They carry it around with them like heavy luggage for years, you must let this go. There are so many successful men and women in the world today who did not apply themselves at school and constantly achieved disappointing results.

The quicker you get off the starting blocks and start learning in your specific field, you'll very soon move quicker and ahead of everybody. If you continuously keep learning new skills, there is no way you cannot.

CHAPTER SIXTEEN

The Best Log You'll Ever Do

We are what we repeatedly do; excellence therefore is not an act but a habit

Aristotle

Why should you write a journal?

Writing a journal is probably one of the most important personal development aids you'll ever have. Unfortunately most people neglect this part of their own development. Why? Because they quite simply can't be bothered, when you write about your experiences and how you overcame them or smashed through them and you write about what you learned. You very quickly see what you don't see if you didn't write it down.

Writing it down is important, don't type it in your computer your journal must be written. Remember *"think in ink."* When you start to log your days and weeks and months, you'll very quickly learn that you are improving in all areas of your life.

The more you write about what's going on in your life and how you took control of your emotions the better. There are several benefits to writing in a journal. Writing in a personal journal allows you to have an outlet for stressful situations in your life. You can release work problems that you would normally keep locked up inside. Writing in a journal gives you the opportunity to reflect on your very own emotions in certain areas and circumstances in your life.

Journals also act as a great tool for reflecting on your emotions, they are great for goal setting and every day write your goals you want to achieve for that day or that week. Journals also help you to develop your communication skills and the more you write about your thoughts and feelings, the quicker it will improve your professional and personal life.

Journals are also an awesome way to capture memories. When you read a journal from an earlier time in your life, you'll realise that once what was a huge mountain to climb back then is just a small molehill now. Journals show you how much you've improved and how things and circumstances that you faced a month or a year ago seemed different, when you didn't have the new knowledge that you have now.

Journals act as a reminder of the things you experienced that you may have forgotten. We all grow and change each year physically and mentally and if you don't log it you'll never know what worked for you and what didn't.

Journals are an awesome way to chronicle your life, your achievements and your Triple D Dragon slaying and improvements. When you've slayed the dragons write about it, write down everything that worked and everything that didn't and learn from it. The art of writing a good journal entry is priceless. Think of it as a stress reliever.

The best thing with writing a journal is there aren't any rules. You don't have to be concerned with spelling or format or content, you just write about what you want. One day it could be about your goals, the next day it could be about your fears or procrastination or even a day when you didn't operate at your best, all because the Triple D Dragon breathed his fear and fire all over you. Or it could be your best day ever, the day when everything came together and you cracked it. You choose what's right for you.

Allow your own thoughts to flow on any subject without fear or repercussion. A journal is a place where you let your thoughts run wild. If you want to keep your journal so you know what you've learned, just divide it into two sections on one side of the paper write what you've learned and on the other side write how you've learned it. I find this process is awesome because so many times you forget how you learned so many different things in your life. Remember when you *"think in ink, you remember it."*

I always use this technique for writing my journal, I always write down things that I've heard or seen that held a strong meaning for me. Or if it's in a newspaper or magazine I'll cut it out and stick it in. I always date my journal entries and if I'm not at home I'll write where I am, If I'm in the garden writing I'll even write my location and I often write about the weather as well.

It's normal to feel like you're not fully achieving your potential in some areas of your life. Keeping a journal will keep you on track and organised in sticking to your goal. I also write about what decisions I've made and how I made them. I find it works when I draw in my journal this can be anything it could a goal you want to achieve or what you'll be doing when you get to your Priceless Life Destination. Remember to honest with yourself with your entries, this is the only way you'll move closer to your goals. The time you take to write in your journal is your time for reflection. Even when sometimes the reality can seem painful, write it down as even unfortunate situations hold a key to your doorway of experiences and you'll automatically learn and grow.

I always end each one of my entries in my journal with a sentence that addresses the following items, how I demonstrated or proved my strengths and weaknesses. How I can improve upon what I did today and how this day helped or hindered my progress.

Don't edit or repress yourself, if your scared write why you were, if you were angry write why you were angry, write it from your point of view. Write about your feelings, I promise this is the juicy stuff that you remember now. However later on down the line you'll forget as you grow and develop.

Whatever and whenever you chose to write in your journal you'll very quickly find that this is a journey of your life and this in itself will make the journaling process a meditative one.

As I said before there are no rules of how to write a journal but here's how I do it and it works for me, if you want to copy my way that's great. See if it works for you.

Here's my instructions and what you'll need

Things You'll Need.

- A Pen.
- A Journal, nothing fancy just a book that you can write your entries in.

My Instructions

- Set time aside every week to write in your journal. Make it a habit, I write in my journal twice a week.
- Make sure you are alone and can't be disturbed. Keeping a journal is all about you and your challenges you are facing.
- Write what you feel.
- Write the date. If you're not at home write your location and the time and put these things at the top of each entry.

- Write about what happened during that day and what you felt.
- Write about what's going on around you.
- Write from your point of view and your thoughts.
- Draw doodles or things to identify with your goals.
- Divide the page into two, what you've learned and how you learned it.
- Cut out articles or pictures or things of interest to keep you on track for your Priceless Life Destination.
- Write down your goals for the next day or that week.

End each journal entry with a sentence that

- Proved your strengths or weaknesses for that day.
- Shows how you can improve upon what you did.
- Shows how this day has helped or hindered your progress.

CHAPTER SEVENTEEN

Never Ever Say Never

You miss 100% of the shots you don't take

Wayne Gretzky

When you develop a new skill called bravery and you dare to live your dreams and break through your own individual barriers that you've imposed upon yourself, you will become the person and attain the things you've always wanted.

Whatever success you have achieved so far in life, have all been down to your ability to push through any difficulties you've faced and keep going until you succeeded.

The biggest dragon you will almost definitely have to slay will be the fear dragon. Slaying a dragon isn't easy it requires valour, audacity, guts and nerve. When you tune into your own power and control your fears and find your own strength a whole new world of possibilities will open up for you.

Have five minutes with yourself everyday and always ask *"if fear couldn't stop me today, what would I do to move closer to my Priceless Life Destination?"*

Again as with all skills you can learn to smash fear and become powerful. When you become powerful and can smash through fear you will automatically build inside that strength and guts and nerve you need to deal with all of life's challenges it will most definitely throw at you.

Remember trouble and challenges will face you all the time, you must become bigger than your challenges and slay the fear dragon. To beat fear we must firstly take a look at our own conditioning we had when we were younger. Remember what I said earlier in the book we've all been domesticated like dogs from an early age.

Stop being caught up in your fears or not being able to do this or that. Stop being sensitive to other peoples opinions that we perceive to be true. These things paralyse us and stop us dead in our tracks, all because we think someone else may not like it. This holds us at gunpoint where we are afraid to move forward and we listen to the dragon that makes up our negative future. Become strong and fearless. The negative future dragon will stop you, it will make you hesitate and procrastinate. It will always be looking out to find an excuse for you to not do it, so it feels safe again.

Remember fear can be caused by ignorance, when we have limited or little information about something our fear dragon loves it, he'll make you avoid taking action on your goals at all costs because he doesn't want to try anything new or different. When we learn more and constantly collect more information, the fear dragon hates it. Because he knows with knowledge comes courage and confidence, he also knows with courage and confidence comes power to slay the dragon and extinguish his flames that have always stopped you in the past.

Just think of driving a car, when you first started you knew nothing. The more you did it the better you became, the more information you collected of when and how to drive you started to become confident. The more knowledge and understanding you collected the faster you became confident and the faster you became confident you gained more knowledge and you destroyed the fear dragon and become efficient and confident at driving.

Don't feel silly or stupid everyone is afraid of something, I mean everyone. If you're reading this book and you say you're not afraid of anything, I can assure you, you are afraid of lots of things. It's totally normal to be afraid of your financial, physical and emotional future survival.

We are all afraid, so how do you deal with it? The person who is bold, brave or intrepid simply moves forward towards their goals in spite of the fear. The crazy thing what I've learnt from my coaching and psychotherapy practise is when you confront your fears and run towards them, your fears simply go smaller and smaller and your confidence and self esteem get bigger and bigger.

I've also found that the opposite happens, if you run further and further away from your fears, your fears become bigger and bigger and your self esteem and confidence gets smaller and smaller.

Check out your fears

Once you have finally realised that you have fears, you must recognise and investigate which areas of your life trigger the fear dragon. To slay the fear dragon you must sit down and have five minutes and write down *"What is it, I'm afraid of?"*

Write down all the big things and the little things that cause you worry or anxiety. Firstly start with the common ones fear of failure or rejection, ridicule or criticism.

Some people are so hung up on how they appear to others that they don't even start because it may not be to their approval. Some people have a fear of failure that they constantly try to cover up their mistakes so they won't look bad. Some people have a fear of rejection; this dragon will stop you from taking action on your goals and you won't even get off the starting blocks

Set fears in order of importance

Once you've made a list of the fears that you think are challenging your thinking and behaviours. Set them out in a list of their order of importance, which fear do you think is holding you back the most? What would be the second and third and fourth?

With your fear in the forefront of your mind write down the answers to these questions.

- How does this specific fear dragon hold me back?
- Is there any good reason why I would want to keep this fear?
- What would be my reward in life for destroying this fear?

When you ask yourself these three questions you automatically open up new and exciting possibilities. You get an understanding of what you are doing and why. When you investigate and analyse your fears, you can then remove them from your life and allow the endless new opportunities to enter.

Remember my story at the beginning of the book. I couldn't knock on big company doors, that was my fear. I knew it didn't make sense, however I knew I should do it but I never did it. As humans we don't make changes in our lives based on what we know, we make changes in our lives based on how it will make us feel.

Let me explain lets take someone who is very much overweight, they know deep down that to lose weight they must eat healthily and exercise. However this person doesn't eat healthily or exercise because of how it will make them feel. They know it's going to be hard work and it's going to be painful.

To face the fear dragon you must practise over and over again and then it becomes a habit. Continuously facing the fear dragon will develop courage and a sense of strength whenever it's needed. To create courage you must first step out of that comfort zone of yours and try something new, different things that will give you that shove we all sometimes need to take that step of faith. If you just keep talking about it then it will never happen, you must start and keep going.

Too often I see clients who are just waiting and waiting for everything to be just right before they make their own move. Remember I said earlier in the book I see the mind as a corridor of different doorways. Behind these doorways we all lock in reference and evidence of our past experiences and we only take action in our lives based on those experiences of what happened in the past. As we move forward towards our goals new a different doors open for us. You've just got to have the strength to go through those doors and grab the opportunities that await you.

We've all heard the saying *"he who dares wins."* Life is always showing you new opportunities and the more you look for it in different ways, the more likely it is to show up.

80% of our Triple D Dragon's self-talk is negative chatter. This negative chatter is always trying to persuade you not to jump out of your comfort zone and have the things you've always dreamed of and desired. When this happens with the fear dragon, focus all of your attention and your intelligence to your goals or Priceless Life Destination. See in your minds eye a clear picture of the person you want to be, acting and behaving and performing in the way you need to, to get the job done.

You will have thoughts of fear and doubt all day long, if you didn't then you wouldn't be human. Those thoughts can help you, when they turn up mess about with them. Change them with thoughts of power and strength and courage. Whatever thoughts you dwell on inside your mind, fear or strength will grow and grow and grow. So be careful.

When you master the fear dragon in your life, you will become happy and successful. The attainment of bravery and valour in your life will mean that fears will no longer play a role in your decision making process. Employ a warrior's mental attitude and slay the dragon. Soon You will be able to set bigger and more challenging goals knowing that you will have the strength and confidence to face any situation or circumstance that life may throw at you.

CHAPTER EIGHTEEN

The Shield Of Significance

We all see the world through our own eyes and we place a certain amount of significance on certain areas of our lives, be careful where you place that significance.

Craig Price

As a truly unique individual of all the millions of people on the planet no one else on earth is like you. It's true that you are one of a kind and being one of a kind makes you extremely special.

We are all the sum total of our own behaviours which becomes our psychology, your physical appearance is easy to define but your psychology is much more complex in its nature and is a result of many different and complex influences that you've experienced in life.

Your brain is continuously logging, storing and processing information all day long and our senses deliver hundreds of thousands of pieces of information to us every second. Our minds cannot cope with all of this information at once. It only has the capacity to process a small amount of the information we see, hear or feel. Which means a huge amount of the information we collect doesn't connect with our conscious thought process.

The question is, how we decide which pieces of information we should be aware of and which pieces of information will remain outside our awareness. Our brain uses a filter a bit like panning for gold it sieves all the stuff or dirt we don't want and lets it flow out of the pan and keeps the golden nuggets. The secret is if we are concentrating on the wrong area of our lives what we perceive to be a golden nugget may well indeed be a pile of dirt. Think of what your own shield represents for you.

Our brain uses this in all areas of our lives from our attitude our beliefs, values, memories, language and characteristics which will form your very own personality. These filters are very effective they help your subconscious to decipher which pieces of information are relevant to you at any one time. This makes your conscious mind very effective because remember its capacity is only very small in relation to the amount of information your brain deals with every second.

So how do these filters work?

They work by deleting, distorting and generalising the information that is being processed by the brain.

Deleting

In order to process the information that our individual personality filters out, information is deleted. The downside to deletion is that information can be missed. Do you ever look around for your keys, and don't see them despite them being right in front of you? This happens to some people more than others but most of us will have experienced it, this is deletion.

Distortion

Our filters can distort information, and this is often based on our expectations of a situation. Sometimes when we expect something we only see those aspects that support our expectations, reinforcing our opinions. This often happens when we have already formed an opinion about someone or something. When a new situation occurs we can distort what is actually happening, to fit what we can expect to happen.

Generalisation

When we generalise we see a summary of an event, this enables us to grasp more information but can also mean that we miss details. We often generalise when we are in a hurry or we are not really paying attention to what is going on.

So we can see how our personality (made up of our attitudes and beliefs etc) can affect the way that we process information and as a result our personality affects our awareness of a situation. Because of this, our personality creates our own reality, and hence our behaviour.

Our personality not only describes our psychology but it also shapes our reality, it is indeed a very powerful aspect of human beings. Each and every reality is truly then a misconception.

Misconceptions

Your opinions are a result then of years and years of rational and irrational objective analysis by you. That analysis is just your own listening's to the Triple D Dragon deleting distorting and generalising all the information to your brain.

The truth is your opinions are a result of paying years of attention to information which you believed and you confirmed you believed it to yourself. While you were doing this confirming what you believed process, you were actually ignoring and pushing away anything in your life that challenged your preconceived notions or things you were certain about.

Have you ever had a conversation at a party with a group of friends and out of the blue you or someone mentioned an old film that you haven't seen for years, lets say it was the Goonies. You all remembered the film; you all laughed about it and you even quoted lines from the film. You all talk that you haven't seen those actors in anything for years.

Then what happens?

You are at home a few days later and you're flicking through the television channels and all of a sudden the Goonies is on. That's strange right? Then the next day you're reading a newspaper and from nowhere it mentions all different films from the 80's and they mention The Goonies.

A few days later you're watching television or at the movies and you watch a trailer and all of a sudden you see some of the actors from The Goonies. You say to yourself *"oh wow. I can't believe it there's the actor from the Goonies."*

So why is it that all of a sudden you see things that are connected with The Goonies? Are there greater powers in the universe that we don't understand trying to tell you something?

Let me explain what's going on, since the party and the conversation you had with your friends. The Goonies has been brought to the forefront of your subconscious mind, it's as if it's looking for it. You've turned over channels on your television hundreds of times; you've seen hundreds of posters and advertising campaigns. You've seen and heard loads of stories about celebrities and you've watched dozens of movie trailers. You've even heard them on the radio in your car.

Until that day of the party you simply disregarded all information and anything to do with the film The Goonies. Out of all your daily routines, behaviours, work patterns and all the different pieces of information you processed every day. You only noticed the bits that were sitting at the forefront of your mind.

A few weeks before the party if one of the actors had been in another film or was on television, you wouldn't have paid any special attention or even noticed it. In other words your blinkers in your subconscious mind weren't switched on to it.

If you're thinking about buying a new car, you suddenly see people driving this car everywhere. If you're having a baby all you see everywhere you go, is babies or ladies that are pregnant. If you've just ended a long term relationship every time you turn on the radio you'll hear songs that remind you of that person.

This is seeing the world through your shield of significance or how I explain to my clients is, imagine you have a sheet of cling film right in front of your eyes and everywhere you look you see the world through the cling film. This cling film only allows the areas that you place certain significance in your life to pass through the cling film and into your brain. It also rejects just like a shield any information that you disagree with or have a personal belief about. New information also tends to be rejected away and disregarded instantly.

All people who have succeeded in life and are successful have learnt to remove this shield and this is a technique I use in my Psychotherapy and Coaching practise. Only when you can see the world and your challenges we face for what they are, what they will be and what they have always been can we truly see it properly.

If it wasn't for the true greats in history who were able to remove their shields of significance when new information came along, our lives would be quite different. We would still believe the earth was flat, we would still believe that a machine that could fly or going to the moon was impossible.

If those people hadn't removed their shields of significance, just think where we would be today. We must reach beyond our own limitations we place on ourselves and remove your own shield of significance now.

Shield Of Significance

- Concentrate on the areas of your abilities you place significance on.
- Check in with yourself on what new ideas you delete out of your life.
- Whatever you bring to the forefront of your mind you'll see.
- Constantly notice what parts of your life you instantly dismiss because it doesn't feel right for you.
- Notice how you delete different people from your life.
- Notice how certain expectations you have of other people make you behave.

CHAPTER NINETEEN

Affirm Your Desires.

What we say about ourselves becomes what we believe about ourselves, what we believe about ourselves becomes what we think about ourselves.
Our thoughts then become our very own reality.

Craig Price

For me this is one of the key principles that changed my life for the better forever. Positive affirmations may sound silly; it did for me when I first started it. However affirmations or affirming your desires are an awesome way to create changes in the way you think and feel in your life.

So what is an affirmation?

An affirmation is basically a sentence that you repeat over and over again continuously until your mind accepts it as the truth. Once this happens the subconscious mind begins to create and shape your life based on the affirmation or the new thought that you have planted in your mind.

As I said earlier when I first started with affirmations all those years ago, I thought it was a complete load of rubbish and it will never work. But I gave it a go. This is what you must do, give it a go. Because when you do I promise you, your life will change for the better.

The more affirmations I did, I quickly realised that all of us regularly repeat affirmations all day long without even knowing we do it. Here's what I mean, how many times do you say to yourself throughout the day such phrases as *"I can't do it"* or *"I'm not good enough"* or *"it will never happen for me."* All of us have and we continue to do this all day long.

When you repeat these phrases over and over again all day long, you eventually believe it to be true because when you're saying it, guess who's listening to what you say? You are. The more you repeat it the more you believe it to be true, it's a bit like an electrical current that goes into your brain and says *"oh well, that's me then, it's obvious it will never happen for me."* Because it's your voice that says it, you believe it and what you believe becomes your reality.

We must change this if you want to succeed in your Priceless Life Destination. Just as we become what we think about we also become what we talk about and if you talk about negative rubbish telling yourself you can't do this or that. Your future will become exactly what you talk about.

When you watch the world strongest man competitions, just before they are about to lift the really heavy weights do they say to themselves *"I'm not going to be able to lift this"* Of course they don't they are psyching their selves up telling themselves they can do it, aren't they?

I'll show you and teach you how to do it and how to make it a daily ritual for you. When you start your day with affirmations it allows you to change your thought process. Your goal is to go from having a negative thought process that looks at all that is wrong in your world, to having a positive thought process. Where you see all the good and positivity in your world.

When you focus on the positive your subconscious mind will create a positive and happier life for you and things that you once thought were impossible or hard, suddenly become possible and attainable. When you focus on the negative and all the things you think you can't or won't do. Your subconscious mind will create negative situations, so you will continue to struggle through life and argue for all of your limitations.

There's a rule with affirmations that I follow and it works, and if you follow my principle it will work for you too.

Affirmations rarely work if they're too long or not properly focused or not directed like a laser beam on its target to create exactly what you want. I also find that they don't work if they are not aligned with the way that you speak.

Here are some affirmation examples that I find would never work for me in a million years:

- I am open to the new positive changes in my life and I welcome them with open arms.
- I am ready to receive all the joy and happiness that the world has to offer me.
- The universe is welcoming me and I'm ready for the new opportunities it will bring.

These are the reasons why these type of affirmations simply don't work

- They are not aligned with the way that you speak; no one normally speaks like this. If you have an affirmation like this your subconscious mind will reject the message and you'll be wasting your time.

- The affirmation is too generic; it isn't focused on anything particular. You must have an affirmation that is clear and straight to the point and clear and focuses on exactly what you want.
- There is no action or power connected to these affirmations and there's no focus on taking the right action or doing the right things or making the right choices.

For the last fifteen years I've been teaching people the power of affirmations and I've seen instant awesome results just by making little changes that anyone can do.

If you want to start a business or get a new job, you must create an affirmation that allows you to start a new job or business. Create an affirmation that allows you to meet the right people who could help you. Design an affirmation that allows you to do the right things to get a new job or start that business.

Here's an example for you if you want to get a new job or start a new business. *"I know what to do to get a new job that pays me £50,000"* (just fill in the amount that's right for you.) or *"I'm doing the right things to start a new business to earn £50,000"* (just fill in the amount that's right for you) or *"I'm meeting the right people to help me to earn £50,000"* (fill in the amount that's right for you) or *"I'm meeting the right people to help me to start my business"*

Make them simple, straight forward and be specific for what you want. You can also measure it because when you get that new job, you'll know how much it pays you.

When you start to work with affirmations have a good look at them and see if they meet the right criteria. Another key principle I find works best for me, is to focus on different areas of your life you want to improve and make an affirmation for each area. However only do about three affirmations at a time. Always check in with your affirmations and if you're not seeing any progress towards your Priceless Life Destination change it. If you are seeing progress, keep them.

When you work with the right affirmations in your life, you will create a new powerful and positive future thinking pattern for yourself; this thinking pattern will help you to succeed. What I quickly found by using affirmations in my life was that, I started to eliminate negative thinking patterns from the Triple D Dragon. My intuition also started to improve and I often caught and still catch myself to this day replacing negative patterns easily and efficiently.

Remember what we say to ourselves on a regular basis ends up becoming the things we believe to be true. If we don't take charge by using affirmations in our lives, very quickly our subconscious mind will pick up on these signals and see them as instructions.

So let's start by instructing the subconscious mind our Triple D Dragon by changing how we communicate, changing the way we talk about our own challenges we face and affirm the new way we want to act and behave by using affirmations.

Positive affirmations and positive thinking techniques help develop a powerful and positive attitude to life. This is essential to success in all areas of your life. When you harness this awesome power you can turn failure around into success and you can take your success to a whole new level that you never thought possible. A positive attitude is the key to success. Let me explain it like this, every thought you think and every thought you've ever had and every word you say or have ever said is an affirmation. All of the Triple D Dragon's self talk and chatter is basically an affirmation. We are continually confirming and affirming subconsciously with our words and thoughts and they are creating our very own life experiences in every moment.

Our beliefs or things that we believe to be true are quite literally learned thought patterns that we developed as a young child. Many of these beliefs work really well for us, but for every one that works well, there's always one that works against us. They are dysfunctional and sabotage us from what we really want. This is The Triple D Dragon breathing his fire all over our lives.

It is so important that we realise that so many of these affirmations that we say to ourselves, the negative rubbish ones are not actually true for us. They are based on things we constructed when we were younger or other people opinions or ideas or other people's beliefs. Only when we take time out of our lives and really examine them fully, do we see they can be exposed for stuff we made up.

The big question is, do affirmations really work?

Yes affirmations work and they work extremely well. You will not find any self help book that hasn't included some form of affirmations and the reason is because they simply just work. The more determined you are to make changes in your life, the more you will accept change and let go of the past and the old you. By choosing to think and say positive affirmations the Triple D Dragon is forced into two reactions, avoidance or reassessment.

Continually repeating affirmations chips away at the old you, it replaces your old negative thought patterns. Affirmations change the way you think and feel about things and when you replace negative beliefs, positive change comes easily and naturally.

The Final Principles For Affirmations

Remember some of the most powerful affirmations you have received in your life came from other people and you quite literally adopted them. These affirmations came from other people when they looked you directly in the eye. Look at your-self directly in the mirror when you say them. When you do this, look directly into your own eyes as you say your affirmation out loud and this will magnify and intensify the quality and the importance of the affirmation and its message upon you. Why? Because it's coming from the most important person in your life and that's you.

I find with my affirmations I say them out loud, strong and with passion and the higher my emotional state the better. The higher your state as you say them the more effective they are. Use powerful words at the end of your affirmation like *NOW* and *EVER AGAIN*. I find at the end of the affirmation on the last word it helps for me when I punch the air and make a fist, even getting angry works really well and focuses me on my goals.

It's really important that you say them out loud and even shout them, find somewhere that is quiet where other people won't see what you're doing. Maybe in a field or even in the woods. When you can say them in rhythm to your movements or foot-steps I find really works. Some people even sing them but if you do sing them, sing them with conviction.

Do not sing them all wishy washy, say or sing them with power, conviction and certainty in your voice and each time you say it, become more and more emotionally attached to it. You must constantly be visualising you Priceless Life Destination of what you want and what it will do for you and what you'll look like when you get there.

Affirm Your Desires

- Say a quick short phrase or sentence that's straight to the point.
- Say it in your own language.
- Shout it out with power, conviction and certainty.
- Say it in rhythm to your footsteps.
- Punch the air and make a fist.
- Visualise your Goal as you're saying it.
- Remember it might feel daft and funny at first.
- Become emotionally attached with what you are saying.
- Make it a daily ritual, do it everyday.

My last words on affirmations are this; if you don't do it then you are simply limiting your success.

CHAPTER TWENTY

Becoming The New You.

"It had long since come to my attention that people of accomplishment rarely sat back and let things happen to them. They went out and happened to things."

Leonardo Da Vinci

To get things done and achieve your Priceless Life Destination you must take action. Things seldom happen on their own.

We all know it can be difficult and hard and we also know it's so easy to be lazy and procrastinate. We must break out of this behaviour and develop behavioural patterns of taking more and consistent action.

Start By Holding Yourself Accountable

Hold yourself accountable for your dreams and goals, when you start by holding yourself accountable, you set your own standards and principles for how you will act and behave. However you must stick to these standards or you'll cheat on yourself and your dreams and rationalise how you don't need to take action. When the social pressure of having to answer to someone else is not there this can happen so find someone you know and tell them your goals. Make sure it's someone who'll tell everyone and make you feel stupid if you don't succeed.

The more people you tell about your goals the harder it will be not to achieve it. For two reasons, firstly you don't want to disappoint them and secondly you know that you're going to have to face up to them and who wants to feel like an idiot.

One of the key factors that hinders people becoming the person they want to be and have all the things they've always wanted is, they don't change their behavioural patterns. They find they continue to do the things they've always done and keep making up excuses, why they just can't have what they've always wanted.

You must change your routines, you must change your habits and you must change your behaviours. The chart on the next pages shows what I mean and how you can apply it to your life. Let's say for arguments sake that your goal is to lose weight and you are 20 stone. Your goal weight is 14 stone so there's 6 stone to lose.

Your behaviours, mindset, routines and habits you currently own have got you to 20 stone right? So to lose weight it makes sense that you must change your behaviours, mindset, routines and habits.

If you don't change them, what will happen? You will continue to put on more and more weight and it will become harder and harder to lose weight, wont it?

So it's imperative to change these patterns that you've installed over your lifetime. Just like everything in life you can learn to change your behavioural patterns, there's a set process to change your patterns and this is what I've found just works.

When you set yourself a goal to lose 6 stone, it's a big goal and when you set yourself a big goal, all of your habits and behavioural patterns that you've already installed start working as quick as they can to put you off. This happens because all you see is the huge goal and all the hard work you've got to do. This is why when you set a big goal; it's so easy to just put it off until tomorrow and as we all know tomorrow never comes.

To stop this from happening, the following principles must be followed. We must break the goal down to 6 steps at one stone weight intervals for each step. If we keep the same behavioural patterns we've currently got at 20 stone we will slip back to 21 stone. So the secret is we must ask ourselves a great question *"what behavioural patterns does a 19 stone person have?"*

Then quite simply adopt those behavioural patterns, you must adopt the patterns of the new you that you must be one stone lighter. If you tried to adopt the patterns of the person 6 stone lighter, it would be too much for you and you would give in and not even start your new life. The chart below will explain it.

You must make a conscious effort to become the new you that you need to be each step in front and take on and adopt all the new behaviours, mind sets, routines and beliefs and thought patterns

You must constantly become the person you will have to be the next step forward towards your goals. The chart on the next page shows how you must do it.

20 Stone	19 Stone	18 Stone	17 Stone	16 Stone	15 Stone	14 Stone Your Goal Weight
Here You Are At 20 Stone starting your journey. To change your weight you must adopt the behavioural patterns of the new you that you will be at 19 stone.	The first step to the new You must take on an 18 stone person's patterns and thought processes	The second step to the new you. You've now taken on board an 18 stone persons mind set, but if you keep that mindset you'll go back to 19 stone	The third step to the new you. You're now making constant changes and realising you must continue to be the new you, that one step ahead	The Fourth Step to the new you You understand that to achieve the goal of 15 stone then your way of thinking must be the same as the 15 stone new you	The Fifth Step To The New You. You only have one step to go to get to your goal weight. however it's really two steps because you've always got to have the mindset of the new you on step in front	Hooray To keep at this weight you must adopt the patterns of a 13 stone person or you'll put the weight back on. Remember you must always be the new you that you want to be to stay where you are.

Start by asking yourself these important questions.

To get to my next step what type of person or new me, will I have to be?

What type of habits must I adopt from that person?

What type of routines must I follow?

What behaviours would the new me in the next step forward be doing?

What would the new me believe in the next step forward?

If there was one thing I could change right now, to be the new me in the next step forward what would it be?

What thought processes would the new me in the next step forward have?

Once you've got your list and you've wrote it all down remember to *"think in ink,"* because if you don't it won't work. Now take action and just adopt those new patterns into your life. Remember you are just adopting the patterns of the new you that one step in front, don't try and adopt the new you at the end of your goal. It's a huge jump and after a few days you'll go back to doing what you've always done and just give up.

Constantly ask yourself whatever your goal is *"what would I have to do or think about to become the new me in the next step closer towards my goals"* and then just adopt those new behavioural patterns. It's really easy because you are only making small changes and anyone can change a little bit, can't they?

Always remember and this is really important, when you stand still and don't take on the new you behavioural patterns of the person in front of you, a slippery slope will appear. You will slip backwards because the behaviours you have now will always drag you back a place along the ladder of success. If you don't upgrade or up skill your behaviours, you'll keep going backwards, that's just how life is. If you do what you've always done you'll always get the same results.

Focus on the how instead of the if's

When you focus on *"what if's"* it really messes with your mind, or what a lot of people say is *"my heads in the shed."* People can spend days, weeks, months or even years thinking about what might happen if they take action. Rather than letting your mind get lost in the wonder of *"what if's"* instead concentrate on the *"how,"* think of all the different ways of how you can do it. How can you solve your problem or attain your goal. Gain more knowledge, do research or even get help from other people. When you concentrate and focus on *"the how"* it puts your sub-conscious to work and it looks for different possibilities for you, it creates that positive mental attitude. Doing this makes it so much easier to take action and stops you waiting and waiting for things to be just right, until you make your move to success.

D.I.L.L.I.G.A.F.

"Dilligaf" Is an acronym and stands for does it look like I give a f**k. This is a technique I use with my clients to allow them to let go of negative areas in their lives. To leave all your past failures or heartaches behind, you must adopt a carefree attitude. The only person who tells you if something is good or bad is you. So you literally make up how you feel towards past and future events, don't you? I see so many people who hang onto what other people think about them, or what they perceive other people think about them. Leaving behind these feelings is easy to do and re-programs your Dominating Delusional Destructive Dragon.

It actually stops the dragon from breathing his fire all over your life, just by saying the word *"dilligaf"* it shocks the dragon and extinguishes his fire. The word *"dilligaf"* acts just like a fire extinguisher to put out that non-stop negative chatter. Alcoholics Anonymous say that you can't change the first thought that comes in to your head, however you can change the second thought, can't you? How quickly can you change a thought? Instantly in fact it's possibly about a millisecond.

When things go wrong as they often will, just say the word *"dilligaf"* to yourself. When you say *"dilligaf"* it's as if you send a signal to your subconscious mind and it lets it go. How does this work? Well it's quite simple, when you let go of the misconceptions you've created by saying the word *"dilligaf."* You create a new reality for yourself of a carefree attitude. When you're carefree nothing can bother you like it did before and the barriers that you once held onto so tightly, drop down.

If you catch yourself saying you can't do something, or you're not confident or you don't have the self esteem or feel inadequate or feel like you want to put it off until tomorrow just say the word *"dilligaf"* and let it go, then change your thought process and take action towards your Priceless Life.

Create A Vision Board

What is a vision board? It's a bit like a scrap book or poster board that you cut out images or quotes from magazines or newspapers or leaflets etc. that inspire you. It really is that simple.

The idea behind vision boards is you constantly surround yourself with images and quotes of what you want to do, have or become. These images could be of a holiday destination, a home you would like to own or a car you have always dreamt of driving. Vision boards add more clarity to your goals or desires. Make sure the images you choose make you feel inspired. There are loads of different methods when creating a vision board and this is what I find works best for me.

Supplies you'll need when creating
your vision board

- A poster board or corkboard or journal, I often use my journal.
- Magazines
- Glue

Before You Begin Your Vision Board

Think about what areas of your life you want to change or the things you want to have such as a new car or house. Then just like setting your goals make a specific area on your vision board for each type of goal. Remember your goals are Personal, Stuff and Financial Goals.

The Five Principle Process For Successfully Creating A Vision Board
Principle 1.

Go through your magazines and see which images suit or match the areas of your goals, don't just use images. Certain phrases are great as well as they could inspire you or you could even use them as your affirmations. Don't worry if the pictures or phrases are too big for the board or journal just fold them up so they will fit.

Principle 2.

Go through the images and just lay them out in order of your wants for each area of your goals. Instinctively you will know what's best for you and where to place the images in order of your goals.

Principle 3.

Glue everything onto the board, you can even add writing with a marker pen if you like.

Principle 4.

Leave a space in the middle of the board for a photo of you and your family and what it will do for you. Remember the *"why"* is your motivating factor and it's the emotions you'll have by looking at it that will cause the motion to get you going and working on your goals.

Principle 5.

Place your vision board somewhere you'll see it often, keep adding bits to it all the time. I use my journal and a board and look at it all the time. If sometimes you feel a bit like giving up, look at your vision board and associate with all those feelings of why you want it. It's a bit like the visualising process.

Start Every Morning The Same Way

Take the first five minutes of every day to dream and think about what you want to achieve. Remember you have the power to change the course of your future and your life. Focus on what you want and go and get it.

We Become What We Think About

Remember to catch yourself doing and saying what you do and say. Take a step back out of the equation and take that check up from the neck up and focus on what you want and why you want it.

Because we become what we think about it's impossible for us to attract success, happiness and great wealth into our lives if everyday we continue to think about poverty and failure and blame our lives on other people and circumstances.

If you are not attracting the life that you want start thinking and dreaming about your new future again. Let go of your current situation or you'll never be able to attract your new destination. Concentrate and focus all of your intelligence and certainty on the life you want to experience and live and make it a life worth living. Your future and your families' future depend on it.

Stop Doing Things That Take Up Your Time & Don't Help You.

Look at how productive you've been that day, if you've not achieved what you wanted remember the Priceless P Principle. I work with lots of executives in their thirties who feel like their own energy, hope and joy and excitement has been drained out of them.

What I often find out very quickly is that they are doing a lot of things that don't really matter, instead of focusing and concentrating on the things they really do want in their lives. Imagine this for a weird concept for a moment, what if you stopped doing the things in your life that really don't matter? How would that change who you are? How much more time would you have to work on your Priceless Life Destination. How would this affect all areas of your life such as your health and well being?

So how do you do it? It's simple; first you need to take a step back. You need to figure out what does matter to you. Sometimes we get so caught up in the moment and don't realise what we are doing and how much time we are wasting.

The second step is to look at what you're doing and who are you spending time with and then remove the stuff from your life that doesn't help. Stop spending all day investing your time and energy in people, ideas, events or anything else that zaps you and your time. In the past few years I've done this process in the principles I've outlined here and the results have been awesome. I simply started by defining what mattered most that day and then removed everything and everyone that didn't fit. Is this easy? Does it take lots of hard work & dedication & motivation? Of course it does, but anyone can do it. You've just got to take that first step and slay the Triple D Dragon.

We all know that anything in life that's worthwhile takes a bit of effort and hard work. All you've got to do is have the drive and the "_why_" or desire to make it happen. I'm so glad I did it because my days are filled with joy and happiness and you can do the same.

See It First

Remember the most successful people see it in their head first, they imagine what they want and desire. If you want to own your own business, see it in your head or in your minds eye. See everything from your office or base to your employees and your very own company logo. Imagine you are signing a contract for a huge deal, see yourself having the new qualities that you need to succeed.

See your website and how it will look and why people will recommend your services to others. Imagine what you'll be wearing and what new people you'll associate with. See it, feel it, hear it, be it, do it and have it all.

Find People That Can Help You.

When we are younger we are told by our parents to watch the company we keep, which are very wise words. The company you keep can destroy you and your dreams. If you have people in your life that keep telling you that you can't do something because of this and that, get rid of them.

You must find people who lift you up make you feel great about yourself. If you are the smartest person in your group, find another group of people to hang out with, you must have people and individuals in your life that you can learn from and will challenge you.

Find people who have a default level that is way out of your reach at the moment, find people whose comfort zones for all different areas of their lives are way above your levels. Find people who have a level of money they cannot go below but for you is so far out of your reach.

When you find these new people, they raise your game they raise your thinking and get you to start thinking in a different way. It is so important that you get this, because when you do you'll develop new strategies that will impact all areas of your life including your finances.

It is so important that you begin to look at your relationships a lot more seriously. Your future relies upon you constantly being connected with the right people in your life. Spend time with people that lift you and make you feel charged with enthusiasm and greatness and not the individuals that drag you down.

Here's My Principles I Use, To Attract The Right People In My Life.

- Check your mobile phone; think when a certain person rings you. Do you want to take their call or do you say to yourself *"oh no, not them again"* if it's a *"oh no"* person delete them from your phone and delete them from your life.
- Look for people who are already where you want to be and find ways to connect with them on a regular basis.
- Remember if you help someone they'll always look for ways to help you.

Get Back To The Basics

What does everyone say when we go off track or don't fly to our full potential "go back to the basics" The basics are the foundations of great-ness aren't they?

Whatever sport you play you must have a good understanding of the basics or you'll never progress, will you? If you play golf and you don't hold the golf club correctly (which are the basics) you'll never hit the golf ball. The most successful people in the world are awesome at the basics, they don't take any shortcuts on anything, they do it the right way. They build strong founda-tions that last.

Remember the basics are a tried, tested and proven formula that works every time. If they didn't they wouldn't be called the basics. If you follow the basics you'll become successful, if you don't then you'll try shortcuts and end up where you don't want to be.

Here's My Principles To Get Good At The Basics

- Write down the basics of your job what you do every-day, then look for ways for you to improve, take steps to improve in that area now.
- Constantly find new ways or tools to improve what you do.
- Step out of your comfort zone and go back to the basics and get it right, stop thinking you know how to do it all of the time, everyday is a school day.
- Practise, practise, practise and then practise some more. The more you do it the better you'll become. An impor-tant thing to remember is that amateurs practise until they get it right but professionals practise until they can't get it wrong.

The Six Letters To Success, ACTION.

It's been said time and time again and studies and tests have proved that super successful people all have one thing in common. They all think carefully about what they want and make decisions quickly. Then they take massive action and carry out their decisions. Whereas unsuccessful people are mainly indecisive and take a long time to think about if they should even make a decision. Because of this they never become wealthy, never reach their aspirations or goals and stay in the same place forever wondering why other people are becoming successful.

Successful people actually try more than other people and the more you try the more you'll triumph. When you become decisive and action orientated, guess what happens? Your life changes and you get out of second gear and go quickly into overdrive. You'll experience more time in your day to get things done than most people around you. You will have more energy and motivation and determination, which will help you to reach your goals faster.

Here's My Principles To Take Action

- Stop putting things off until tomorrow, ask yourself this question *"Is there one good reason why I don't want to do it."*
- Start small, when you look at a big goal it puts you off immediately. So start small and do the first thing you need to go forward on your goals.
- Always remember <u>*"WHY"*</u> you want this goal because it's the emotions that causes the motion for you to take action.

Become A Person Of Super Self Discipline

To become successful in any area of our lives we must attain self discipline. All of us have felt like we just can't be bothered at some time in our lives or when we wake up in the morning and it's raining we just don't feel like getting up and going to work or going to the gym. You know what; there are times when even I don't feel like doing the things I need to. If you didn't you wouldn't be human would you?

But I push past my feelings and The Triple D Dragon and just do it anyway, I do this because I understand to become successful I must practise self discipline. You must be willing to delay or put off that ten second fix you get so you can reach your goals. You must be prepared to push away the feelings of *"I'm just not right today"* or *"I just don't feel like it today."* Only then will you be able to focus on your Priceless Life Destination.

Obtaining self discipline requires you to master your feelings, your self control and your own self direction. Successful people make a habit of doing the things that unsuccessful people don't like to do on a regular basis. Now this is the crazy thing, successful people don't really enjoy doing the things they don't like to do. However they do them anyway because they know there is always a price to pay to attain your goals and sometimes it can be inconvenience.

Are you willing to pay the price? Are you willing to be inconvenienced? You cannot become successful without being inconvenienced, there's always a price to pay.

You must become a new person who just gets up and does it whether it feels good or not. You must do this and focus all of your efforts on this, because your future depends on it.

Here's My Principles To Self Discipline

- Write down your priorities and keep them where you'll see them everyday.
- When you feel discouraged or you can't be bothered, look at your list and do what you've got to do to get where you want to.

- Stop thinking too much about it and just start, if you don't get off the starting blocks you'll never get there.
- Make a habit of doing the things you don't like to do.

Look After Yourself

Successful people take great care of themselves, they know that you must put your health at your utmost importance because without it you can't do anything. They totally understand that it won't matter if they become a billionaire if they aren't around to enjoy it.

When we are healthy we think differently, being healthy plays a huge role in our ability to think creatively. I find after intense exercise I'm ready to take the day on and all the challenges it may bring.

The more exercise you do that pushes your comfort zones, the more you breathe deeply and the deeper you breathe the more oxygen you create pumping through your body. If you eat healthily, eat lots of fruit and vegetables and high protein, low fat foods and drink loads of water you'll attain that zing in your step and have more energy and vitality than others to accomplish more in your day.

Here's My Principles To Stay In The Lean Zone

- Make your health your number one importance, without it you can't do anything.
- Eat a healthy balanced diet, full of fruit and vegetables
- Drink lots of water.
- If you don't enjoy going to the gym find a hobby that you'll enjoy.
- Every time you exercise push your limits, this will aid in your nights sleep.

- Think like a cow graze often and eat little portions. Eat five times a day and don't eat any carbohydrates after 7.30pm.

Believe In You & Your Abilities.

Super successful people have massive amounts of belief and confidence in themselves and their abilities. To become successful and have others believe in you, when you don't believe in yourself is a recipe for failure.

It's almost impossible for others to believe in you, if you don't believe in yourself, isn't it? If you want to move up to the higher plains of success you must develop a plan of how to become a person with great confidence. For a lot of people confidence comes with knowledge, the more you know the more you'll grow and the more you grow the more your confidence will flow.

Remember who loves to destroy your confidence? The Triple D dragon is always there telling you that you're not good enough. He's always telling you nobody wants you or your products. He's always telling you that you're not smart enough. He's always telling you that if you failed before you'll fail again. When you know more, you'll automatically grow more. For lots of people it's only the knowledge they lack, or the understanding in a certain area that is stopping them believing in themselves.

Here's My Principles To Believe In Yourself

- Educate yourself in your own field or industry, the more you'll know the more you'll grow.
- Stop listening to The Triple D Dragon.
- Often you are the only one who knows what you don't know.
- Act as if you know, say things with confidence.

See The Opportunity In Every Difficulty & Not The Difficulty In Every Opportunity.

The most successful people in the world are nothing but problem solvers. Life is all about solving problems every day, week, month and year we will inevitably have problems. Even if you don't go for your goals or make a decision to be better and improve you and your surroundings you'll have problems.

Just as you'll have problems when you don't set yourself goals you'll have problems when you do set yourself goals. We will always face new difficulties throughout our own lives. We must look for the opportunities in the difficulties and not the difficulties in the opportunities.

Just ask yourself this question "*do you see every setback as an opportunity or not.*" Keep looking, there's always something you can learn and improve upon.

Remember for every problem there's a solution if that wasn't true we wouldn't be able to fly all over the world or have torches and light bulbs to see in the dark would we?

I often find asking someone else's opinion always helps, when you see it from a different perspective you'll see something different. Ask children for solutions, who know's they might just surprise you.

Here's My Principles To Be A Problem Solver.

- Remember for every problem there's always a solution.
- There's always more than one solution to a problem.
- Think differently be open and creative at all times.
- Ask other people for their help, things often look easier from someone else's point of view.

- If you think you can't find a solution, think again and go back to the drawing board.
- Ask children how they would tackle this challenge.

Find A Coach, Mentor Or Join A Mastermind Group.

A mastermind/mentoring group is a group of like minded people that meet on a regular basis to share ideas and solutions on problems and hold their selves accountable for their goals and future success.

You will all work together on your own goals and it's that sense of camaraderie that you're all on it together, that will hold you accountable to keep taking action on your dreams

Through my mastermind and mentoring groups I've had the opportunity to help people reach their goals quicker than they could imagine. Through my mastermind/mentoring groups people succeed faster because they are constantly working on new ways and ideas all the time to become successful.

I currently facilitate mastermind/mentoring groups that meet in person, by phone, webinars, seminars and even by video and cd. If you would like more information on how to join, and make your dreams a reality at a fraction of the cost of seeing me in one of my coaching sessions. Simply visit www.billionairebeliever.com

Learn more about my mastermind/mentoring groups by contacting me. www.billionairebeliever.com or craig@pricelesssuccess.co.uk

CHAPTER TWENTY ONE

It's Only Over When You Say It Is.

*Defeat doesn't finish a man, quit does. A man is not finished
when he's defeated.
He's finished when he quits.*

Richard M Nixon.

Just take five minutes right now and think of all the things you have in your life. Everything that you had to work hard for was definitely worth it, wasn't it? Everything that you've got in your life to this moment, everything you've ever succeeded to obtain is just you gaining perseverance in your life until you've attained it.

When you make a decision to leave all your excuses and limitations and perpetual Monday mornings behind you, know exactly what you want and why you want it. Smash through the barriers that have always held you back before and continue to make improvements on yourself every day in every way, notice what works and what doesn't. Take action on the things that work and what don't, you will very quickly obtain all the things you've always desired.

The number one critical principal is to never give up; so many people give up just when they are so close to greatness. This is one of the key reasons why people just don't become successful. Here are the principles you don't know about how your Dominating Delusional Destructive Dragon works. These principles could be destroying everything in your life.

When you don't feel confident you don't do the stuff you need to do. When you don't do the stuff you need to do because of lack of confidence, your Triple D Dragon goes into overdrive. It's listening out to everything you say to yourself all day long and storing it for another time in your life to say to you *"we had no confidence last time, so it won't be any different this time."*

It's a bit like an electric signal going straight to your brain and electrocuting and frazzling your brain to condition it, so you won't ever do it again. Your Triple D Dragon will then talk to you and say *"why even try because that happened last time and it will definitely happen again."* As humans we take this on board and with taking this on board you install inside your Triple D Dragon that you have no confidence to do it. The Triple D Dragon never forgets this, especially when you do it again and again and again.

Our confidence we have, is linked with the things and associations that we've hung on to in our past. It's a bit like carrying around loads of luggage with us for no reason what so ever. You wouldn't carry around with you loads of bags and suitcases around with you every day if you didn't need them, would you?

I want to share with you how to attain more confidence, because when you become more confident your results will follow. What results you ask? The results you'll need to have the things you've always wanted and desired.

I've noticed, just as I'm sure you have that so many people aren't as confident as they could be or as confident as they want to be in so many different situations in their lives. These areas could be standing in front of a group of people, which is one of the most common areas where people find themselves not very confident. It maybe meeting new people and starting a conversation, it may even be in sporting activities where other people are watching you. Whatever the area that's right for you. I'm certain that however confident you are right now, there are times when you'd like to have that little bit more confidence wouldn't you?

The following three ideas I want to share with you now, will give you the mental understandings and processes to give you confidence when you need it.

1. Confidence Principle.

Have you noticed how much more confident people are when they aren't themselves? What do I mean by this, well I'm sure you've noticed that when people are at a fancy dress party and dressed in fancy dress they act a lot more confident, don't they? Even a really shy person will suddenly act as the life and soul of the party all because they are wearing a fancy dress costume. It's as if they've taken on a brand new identity. I've noticed that seems to work even more when the person is wearing a mask.

2. Confidence Principle.

When clients come to see me for confidence issues, I always ask them when they ever felt confident in their lives. I often get the same response. They tell me when they have a set plan to follow they feel less stressed or if they just feel like they are copying someone else who can do it they also feel less stressed. They feel when they just copy someone else's movements or instructions of what to do it felt easy.

3. Confidence Principle.

People find that when they are in the zone and they are totally concentrating on what they are actually doing they perform better. They find if they are letting their mind wonder and start think-ing of the ending of what they must do, they feel they come out of the zone. Sports people use this all the time staying in the zone, when they allow their minds to think of other things like lifting the trophy or making their winning speech they lose their nerve and their edge and end up way down the leader board. We've all heard this time and time again, haven't we? All sports people have all said the same thing if they would have only stayed in the moment they performed at their highest level, when they got ahead of themselves and started thinking about winning and lift-ing the trophy, they lost their nerve and also the tournament.

These three awesome processes we can use to have that new confidence we want, but more importantly when we really want it. So how do we use these strategies, it's just like everything else you have to learn to do it and here's how.

Principle 1, the fancy dress party clothes principle. We can either wear a gorilla costume so no one will recognise us, but that's not very practical is it. Or we can imagine we are wearing the clothes or fancy dress costume. Now here's a very important question, when we are wearing the fancy dress clothes it's only the way we are imagining we will be seen differently isn't it. So there's really no difference from actually wearing them than imagining you are wearing them. it's only in your head how you feel about it and who tells you if something is good or bad. You do, don't you.

So let's play with this idea, is there any favourite clothes you like to wear that make you feel confident or feel good about your-self. Do you have a special item of clothing that makes you feel like a million pounds and feel like you could almost do anything? We often hear of sports people who have lucky or magic socks or trousers because they feel it gives them good luck. All of us have something that we feel makes us feel better or gives us good luck, for me I have a lucky key ring it's a brass penguin and I rub his stomach for good luck.

I also have a certain suit that makes just feel great about myself. From the moment I wear it, I feel more confident as I know that suit is subconsciously connected to an earlier experience I had when I was very confident before and succeeded in one of my goals. Just like with sports people we hear of footballers wearing the same lucky socks, because they wore those socks in the past when they scored an important goal. So if you need to be confident either wear the previously connected garment or imagine yourself dressed in them. Because as I said before, it's only inside our heads why and how we feel confident, isn't it?

Principle 2, copying someone else better than you is a great way to start to become more confident. A fabulous question to ask yourself is *"who do I know who does this well and has all the confidence that I want"* it's as easy as that, then just copy what they do, that's called modelling. Just copying what someone else does who's better than you are. Let's say you were going to a really important meeting and you needed to be on you're "A" game, a great question I ask myself is this "who do I know who possesses the confidence that I need today. Who is the person *and what attributes do they posses that I need today to help me?"*

Then I imagine that person, now it could be a celebrity or a movie star or even a friend or family member, but they must have that certain something that I need on that day. Then quite simply, I close my eyes and imagine them holding the meeting for me doing what they do, walking how they walk, talking like they talk and acting how they act. I watch what they do and how they behave and I copy it. I also imagine they are on my shoulder in the meeting talking to me, guiding me, telling me what I must do next. I also imagine they are whispering their magic in my ears and coaching and guiding me along to my own greatness. Telling me how to hold myself, talk with conviction and power and to speak clearly and precisely. This works every time for me and I know it will do the same for you as well.

Principle 3, when you're in the zone and don't concentrate or focus your attention on anything else, you just get the job done. So use principle number 2 with principle number 3 and you will become confident. Only focus on, only think about, and only imagine you are in the moment of it happening. How many times do you hear people say *"right that's it. I've got to get in the zone now?"* Well if you don't get in the zone or in the sweet spot then you won't be confident. Stop thinking about what your outcome will be, because when you do you are stopping it from happening. You must learn to let it go and let it grow only when you can do this, will you achieve total confidence.

When we act and behave much more confidently we become more confident. Confidence is something that we all need in so many different ways in so many different times. When you achieve confidence and I mean total confidence you will have the secret ingredient to propel you to your dreams.

To conquer your world you must first conquer your mind and 80% of your emotions are determined by how you talk to yourself. Your attitude or confidence is shaped by your influences and associations. Your subconscious mind creates your confidence levels on your own limiting beliefs of what you feel you can do or not do. So the things of your past hold you down, if you let go of your misconceptions of how confident you think you are, then you cannot be dragged down any longer if your not holding on to it can you.

Find new and exciting ways to compliment other people, why? Well when you think negatively about yourself, far too often you will pass those feelings onto other people in the form of gossip or insults. This recurring negative pattern will destroy your life and your confidence. You must get into the habit of praising other people and what they've done. Instantly put a stop to all of that back stabbing and gossip and start by making and taking a real effort to be nice and compliment people around you.

There are lots of wonderful things that will happen when you do this. Firstly people will start to like you and you'll build confidence, when you do that and start to look for the best in other people, you will automatically bring out the best in you as well. This will help you to talk to other people and will raise your own confidence levels through the roof.

As with all great ideas and sayings the simpler the better and I want you to remember this every single day. You have not achieved what you wanted to in the past all because you said to yourself *"that's it, I've quit."* I know it sounds simple, but it's the truth when you give in or quit it really is over.

If you had not quit earlier on your goals in the past, you would have achieved them, wouldn't you? So it's simple, just stop quitting on you and your dreams. Start by becoming persistent and consistent. I think that Sylvester Stallone said it best in the film Rocky Balboa *"Its not about how hard you can hit, it's all about how hard you can get hit and keep moving forward. That's how winning is done."*

When you get to the point of giving in you must keep going and going. Sylvester Stallone consistently tried over and over again to get into the film industry with no joy. He was trying to become an actor and had knock back upon knock back. No agent or filming studio would take him as a serious actor every audition he went to they just didn't want to employ him as an actor. One day he was at a casting for a film and when he left the casting directors office he told them he wrote and would they be interested in looking at his manuscript. The director said they would have a quick look at it. Sylvester says this was the turning point of his career, now at this point Sylvester Stallone hadn't wrote anything at all. He got to work and that's when he wrote Rocky. He locked himself away for three days and wrote the story to Rocky and pitched it to the movie industry

Now the story goes like this, when Sylvester did show it to them they loved the story and wanted to buy the film from him for $125,000. At this time Sylvester Stallone had no money, he even had to sell his wife's jewellery and his dog to stay alive. He turned down the money they offered him for the script because he said if he sold it to them, then he would have to be the leading role and play Rocky.

They told him he was a nobody in the film industry and no one would want to see a film without a leading actor. They didn't want him to play the lead role in the film they wanted Burt Reynolds or Ryan O Neil to play the part of Rocky. Sylvester told them no, if he wasn't the playing the leading role then they couldn't have the script. This went on for a few weeks and each time the film company increased their offer to buy the script, but still they didn't want Sylvester to play the leading role. At one stage they offered him almost $500,000 for just the script and for him not to play Rocky.

Sylvester persisted and persevered and finally they said he could play the leading role but for a minimal fee. Sylvester agreed and asked if it was a success, could he have royalties from the film. A year later Rocky won the Oscar at the film industry awards and he became an overnight success. His winning speech at the Oscar's mentioned his earlier life and how all the film studios and casting agents had turned him down again and again. Just as the film Rocky was all about an underdog, so was Sylvester Stallone's real life and winning Oscar speech.

If it wasn't for his perseverance, stick ability and never give in attitude then Sylvester Stallone wouldn't be the superstar he is today. We all know that every single man and woman in the world today has and always will have to withstand and experience huge misfortunes and difficulties on their way to success. The only thing that made these people get what they wanted was their own ability to stick with it. Without this stick ability principle then success will not come knocking on your door.

The one principle that guarantees success each and every time with a doubt is the willingness, commitment and dedication to stick with it. Even when everything inside you and everyone around you tells you to stop, quit or just do something else. If you persist, you will almost undoubtedly succeed every time. This certain principle will only work for you when you get your head space in the right place and know exactly what you want and are totally committed, not to quit until you achieve it.

Remember your goal or Priceless Life Destination is only truly over when you decide to quit and that's it.

Never Ever, Ever, Ever, Give Up.

Successful people just don't give up ever; the word quit isn't in their vocabulary. It doesn't matter how tough it gets in any area of their lives they don't give in.

I see it all the time in my children's sports days, as soon as another child overtakes them in a race they give up and look disheartened. How many times have you found yourself doing the same? How many times have you given up on your dreams?

The pathway to greatness is a rough road, that's why so few never finish the journey. If you want to reach your goals, dreams and desires you must never give up on yourself. Each and everyday you must do things that bring you closer to your dreams. I say to all of my coaching clients *"If it doesn't hurt, it doesn't work."* You know that to reach your goals it's going to cause you some discomfort, but if you don't go forward into that discomfort you'll never achieve your goal.

It's Only Over When You Say It Is.

- Write down all the things you've given up on before
- Ask yourself *"Did I give up on this for the right reasons."*
- If not revaluate and start it again.
- Stop and smell the roses now and again. Sometimes we feel like giving up because we are feeling overwhelmed, get out and about in the fresh air. Charles Darwin said his best thoughts came to him when he was walking in the countryside.
- Remember, if it doesn't hurt it doesn't work.
- Think like a fancy dress party and wear clothes that make you feel and act confidently.
- Copy someone else you admire
- Stay in the zone, focus on the now and not the outcome.

Conclusion

Make It Happen For You

You have now learned all of the 21 Priceless Success Principles, by regularly working on and practising your Priceless Success Principles in this book, you will be able to accomplish more in the next few weeks, months and years than most people could accomplish in 10 different lifetimes.

If there is one principle I can give you to become successful instantly. The principle of taking action straight away would be the key ingredient. Without taking action on your goals you'll always be sitting around waiting for your life to change.

I have learned that if you move towards your Priceless Life Destination with confidence and dare to live the life you've always imagined for yourself. You will pass through an invisible barrier that's always been there, it's something that you've never seen before. Allsorts of magic will happen and you'll begin to see windows and doors of opportunity that you didn't notice before.

Remember this; there cannot be a problem without an answer or solution. So if things are bad for you right now there's always an answer somewhere. Every winner was once a whiner, complaining about their circumstances and lack of opportunities.

Life is made up out of choices and decisions and you will whether you consciously decide to or not, make a decision after reading this book, if you're going to apply The Priceless Success Principles to your life. If you don't make a decision to apply these awesome principles, the life you've already got and the habits and routines you've already formed will have dominance over your life and you'll quite simply go back to your old life.

Only when you follow the Priceless Success Principles will you master your life. Here are the Priceless Success Principles for living your life the way you've always wanted to and having the things you've always dreamt of owning and leading an awesome life.

1. Your Priceless Life Destination

Remember to think in ink, write it all down if you don't I promise it will not change. Only 5% of people in the world have clear, specific and defined goals. That 5% of people who set those goals earn ten times more than the remaining 95% combined.

So it's official, setting goals just works. Follow my process and it will work for you too.

- Decide what you really want in all the areas of your life.
- Write them down in detail.
- Set a start and a finish date for your goals.
- Make a list of everything you need to do to achieve them.
- Find out what's always stopped you in the past, remove the mental roadblocks and invisible barriers.
- Follow my principles for destroying the barriers.
- Develop a plan of action and prioritise in order of importance starting with the fist step.
- Remember the Triple D Dragon is not on your side he's your enemy.

- Once you've completed the first step do the second then the third and the fourth and so on and so on.
- Reward yourself along the way, if you don't you could get bored.
- Don't procrastinate, take action immediately even if it's for just ten minutes just do it now.
- Do something every single day to continue to move forward to your goals without fail.

Do this process with any of your goals right now, it's fun and exciting and gets you in the taking action zone where all the greatness happens and you'll achieve more than you ever thought possible.

2. Why Oh Why Oh Why

It is so important to find your "_why's,_" the reasons why you want to achieve your Priceless Life Destination. If you don't have enough reasons of why you want it you won't go after it. It's the emotion that creates the motion in your life that moves you forward to your goals, so tune in with your emotions and become connected with what you want emotionally. Think of all the reasons you want your goal and what it will do for you. Only then can you truly obtain your desires.

3. The Invisible Giant

To truly become successful you must remove the barriers that are between you and your goals. These are only self imposed limitations that you have installed from a child. These beliefs of your mental barriers or road blocks are locked away inside your unconscious mind. You must find these barriers and explore and investigate them and remove the obstacles in your path.

4. Take Control Of Your Remote Control.

If you feel like you're out of control and you allow life, circumstances and other people to lead you down their pathway you will never attain you Priceless Life Destination. To become successful you must push the correct buttons on your remote control, if life isn't where you want it to be, push a different button take control now.

5. See It As Done & Dusted.

We become what we think about on a regular basis, start by becoming a future orientated person set goals in the future, constantly ask yourself what you must do to become the new you.

6. The Dominating, Delusional, Destructive Dragon.

The nickname I use for that little voice inside your head. Just like you protect your home from thieves, if you don't protect your life from the Triple D Dragon it will steal your life. A lot of the non stop chatter will be about you and your own abilities and the way it makes you feel. Make sure that you slay your own dragon and replace them with positive and consistent new empowering beliefs.

7. My T.F.A.B. Formula

Changing the way you think about success and noticing why you've always done what you've done before is and always will be down to the way we have been conditioned in our lives. What we saw, what we heard and our own experiences play a huge part of the laws of manifestation. We must address the viruses we've installed into our minds, become clear about this principle and you will succeed.

8. I Can't Do That!

How many times do you say to yourself *"I can't do it,"* but when you give it a go just by magic you find that you can. The only reason you say you can't do it, is because you've not learnt to do it. Success is a skill that anyone can learn. Now is the time to learn and when you do, you'll instantly become confident.

9. The Naysayers & The Yaysayers

Your own individual choices of people that you choose to be around will have an enormous effect on your life and your future success. Make a decision today to only associate with people who you can learn from or admire or would like to be like. This is one of the key principles to success. Whoever you hang around with you will adopt their characteristics without you even knowing.

10. Flexible People Never Get Bent Out Of Shape.

You must be clear about what your Priceless Life Destination is going to be, but remember to achieve it you must become flexible. Things will always come up along the way to challenge us and you must be willing to always try a new way or approach to get to your goal.

11. Your Action Plan

The more you plan the more you will succeed it's as simple as that. When you can master the skill of planning you and your day, you will be able to accomplish the biggest of goals you never thought possible. It doesn't matter what education you've had a well devised plan will always get you to your goals quicker than the smartest whiz kid without one.

12. Get Organised.

When you can manage your time well, you'll double your productivity. Setting your priorities in order of importance is essential to becoming successful, or you'll just get bogged down and stay in the same place. This one principle will save you months or even years of wasted time that you'll never get back.

13.The "M" Word.

To become successful you must refresh your motivators daily and continue to associate with all the feelings everyday of what you'll personally achieve by achieving your goals. Constantly find films or music or even cuttings from newspapers that inspire and motivate you to succeed.

14. Think About It.

See your new life that you want to live, just like a movie in the future and you are directing the movie and attracting all the things into your life that you want. See yourself as if you have already achieved your own greatness and you are living your dreams. Create these wonderful mental images into your life everyday and you will attract everything you've thought about.

15. Do The Do Everyday.

When you become consistent and persistent in pursuit of your goals they will become a reality quicker than you can imagine. Taking action is a skill that can be learnt. Taking action everyday is essential to your success, if you don't, you'll stay in the same place forever and keep arguing why you've never achieved your goals.

16. The Best Log You'll Ever Do.

When you keep a record of how you've changed and how you've developed and how your own individual thought processes have changed. You'll very quickly see that you are becoming the person you need to be. If you don't write it down, time will pass by so quickly and you'll just take it all for granted. You won't notice this new person you've become. You'll miss the transformation and you won't even remember how you used to behave. Write it down, magic happens when you write things down.

17. Never Ever Say Never.

The biggest dragon you will almost definitely have to slay is the fear dragon. When you have limited or little information we fear making changes, by learning more we become powerful and confident. This one principle will slay the biggest of dragons inside your head.

18. The Shield Of Significance.

Each and every single one of us are totally unique individuals and we all see the world through our own eyes and we place a certain amount of significance on a certain area of our lives. Whatever you focus on you will attract into your life, be careful what you focus on, the shield of significance doesn't care if it's good for you or not.

19. Affirm Your Desires

All day long we repeat to ourselves inside our heads whether or not we can do something, this internal communication with yourself will become your very own reality. Continually repeating affirmations chips away at the old you and reprograms your subconscious mind and helps develop a powerful and positive mindset.

20. Becoming The New You.

When you can learn the powerful principle of becoming the new you that you must become to attain your priceless life, your life and circumstances will change automatically. You have deep within you an awesome power to become the new you that you must be to become successful; this new you power will bring you your goals and everything you want and need in your life faster than ever before.

21. It's Over When You Say It Is.

One of the biggest success factors beyond any doubt is continuing to move forwards towards your goals, dreams and aspirations. Even when everything seems to be against you, this one success trait will help you gain your utmost desires quicker than you could have imagined. Far too often so many people give up when they could have had everything, if they would have just held in a little while longer.

So there you have it, my Priceless Success Principles a proven, tried and tested formula for success. I promise you by following each principle and regularly reviewing and practising my principles you will live the life of your dreams and attract all of the things into your life you desire and deserve. Remember that no one is like you. You are a unique individual with a light so bright inside just waiting to shine, it would be a tragedy to not let it shine to its full brightness or potential.

Unleash your awesomeocity to the world.

To Your Continued Priceless Success, today, tomorrow and forever

Craig

Your Next Step

You can now do what 95% of the population do, read this book and say to yourself "*wow that was great I learnt loads of great ideas and I'll start it all tomorrow.*" You and I both know that's never going to happen because tomorrow never comes..

Chances are you only have a 5% chance of using the principles in this book to Attract Your Priceless Life Destination. Why? Well the answer is simple, because you're human. It's true you can use this book as a springboard to achieving everything you've ever wanted in life, success, fulfilment and money or even love whatever it is you're lacking right now. Only 5 out of 100 people who read this book will actually be able to get the things that they want out of life.

This is because we inherently have built in barriers that keep us from getting the things we really want. We have self imposed restrictions that hold us back and no matter what we try unless we can identify and destroy these barriers, we'll never truly live the life we've dreamed.

Craig Price over the last 14 years has transformed thousands of peoples lives in his Psychotherapy and Life Coaching Sessions to give clients the knowledge, self-understanding, motivation, skill and mind-sets to get everything they want out of life and their careers. Craig has helped people to fulfil there most far reaching dreams by showing people proven techniques and strategies of getting people from where they are to where they want to be.

And now it's your turn

Let Craig help you, shatter and smash your barriers. I know there's a void of some kind in your life, if you're human there has to be. Just click on.

www.pricelesssuccess.com

www.pricelesstherapy.com

www.pricelessweightloss.com

www.billionairebeliever.com

Whatever areas of your life you need help with Craig can identify those areas that could be holding you back. Over the years Craig has helped thousands of clients and he can do it for you too.

If you would like to buy the 5 CD'S that accompany this book please email craig@pricelesssuccess.co.uk or visit www.pricelesssuccess.com for availability and price.

CPSIA information can be obtained
at www.ICGtesting.com
Printed in the USA
BVOW06s1106030517
483079BV00016B/208/P